The Reclining Master
Awaken!

"ONE MINUTE TO HEALTHY ESTEEM"

Tamir Qadree
(With Gary)
www.esteemnow.com

THE RECLINING MASTER "AWAKEN!"

"ONE MINUTE TO HEALHTY ESTEEM"

"Self-esteem goes to the level of being!"

By Author, Speaker and Dynamic Life Coach

TAMIR QADREE

WWW.ESTEEMNOW.COM

Cover Design by Flynn Design

ISBN: 0-9658228-2-6

Esteem Now, Inc.
6333 Pacific Ave 525
Stockton CA. 95207

888-217-8664

www.esteemnow.com

Printed in United States of America

A PUBLICATION OF
MORE HEART THAN TALENT PUBLISHING, INC.
6507 PACIFIC AVE, SUITE 329
STOCKTON, CA 95207
800-595-6632

Dedication

To all the little children of the world,
"Live life, and remain a child at heart".

To Ashani, Tajuddin, Amari, and Ismael
My child angels!

To The Mighty Elements;
Earth, Wind & Fire

To all those who are seeking a life of
Peace, love, happiness, success and wealth.
May your yearning be fulfilled and,
May life reward you with the Best of the Best!

Foreword

It is my privilege and my great pleasure to introduce you to the information you will discover in this empowering book.

I met Tamir in a manner that was very synchronistic. This encounter was not an accident but came at a time when this book was merely an idea, which has now come to fruition. This ability to turn the vision of his ideas into tangible results is the very reason that you deserve to integrate the wisdom Tamir collected through his own personal journey while he was becoming an agent of change into your consciousness as you continue your journey of growth and personal development.

As you read this material, it will become obvious to you that Tamir is not delivering theory; he is delivering Universal truth that could only be gained by going through his own personal challenges. This book will allow you to feel rather than think as you are changing your beliefs about yourself and will assist you with developing a sound foundation in your heart about who you are becoming.

Tamir knows that confidence is how you feel about something you do, while self-esteem is how you feel about yourself. So open your heart and prepare yourself to be in the hands-free zone as you read this book of wisdom. The Reclining Master, "Awaken" One Minute To Healthy Esteem, will allow you to take quantum leaps in your life to become the person you deserve to be!

Jeffery Combs
President, Golden Mastermind Seminars, Inc.
www.GoldenMastermind.com

Appreciations

Thanks from me go the *Creator* of all things, seen and unseen. I thank that force that many call *God,* for my endurance and yearning for the peace of mind and happiness that I now enjoy, and I will always look forward to with every dawn of a new day. I give untold thanks and appreciation to *my parents,* who gave me life. To my father, I am eternally grateful for the determination he instilled in me, and to my mother for the compassion and fairness, which she nurtured in me. To *Theresa Qadree,* who gave me the wonderful blessings of loving and gifted children. I thank*, Ashani, Ismael, Tajuddin and Amari* for their unconditional love and support. No matter what was happening, they are the picture of happiness I see in the magical world of my imagination, as I explore the things that we plan to do and places we plan to go. I thank my friends *Chu Straughter, Adio Mangrum, Ari Sanders, Dr. Ed Zeiter, Greg Somerville* and many more that have inspired me over the past two years. *Scott Lijon*, my oldest brother, has been endless support and helped out when I did not have a cent to buy even gas; I thank him for all he is, and all that he will become, which I know will be something great. I send special, loving thanks to *Nnika Hanserd* who has been a friend, supporter and a dynamic human being in my life; thanks for your empowering words of encouragement. I am hard pressed to think of anyone with the consistent encouragement that *Nnika* has given me. I would like to thank and show great affection for my friend *Loraine Beasley* who endured my breakthrough with me, and supported me. *Loraine* is a gentle soul, with love and affection for all life. I thank *Austion Behn and Thomas Harris,* both of whom has always been sources of endearing support when things got downright ugly and times were difficult. I give a special shout-out to my friend of 31 years, *Sherman Williams*, my high school friend and one of my biggest fans. To my friend *Kim King*, I send thanks and blessing to her family for the words of life and enthusiasm that she has shown for my work and its production over the past 7 years. I also thank *Lillian Hamilton and Vincent Haynes* for their support and for just being good friends, good business associates, and for showing understanding in times of despair. To my *Aunt Pearl,* I give thanks for the peace and tranquility that she brings to my life. She has been valuable and understanding throughout the years, she encouraged me to write and speak when no one else did. In fact, more than any other factor outside of myself, it was her words in November 1994, that prompted me to start writing. Therefore, I pray that all her heart's desires be met speedily. I give a special thanks to *Erica Combs* for being the dynamic person that she is, and for her lending hand, and imagination to the final production of this work. I thank *Jeffery Combs* for being a teacher, friend, coach, mentor and someone who cared enough about me and about others, to tell it like it is. In part, because of *Jeffery Combs*, this book has been brought to the world, for the world, in a relatively short period of time. His tapes, books, cd's and seminars are heart felt and truly amazing; I will never forget and will always cherish the experiences of a friend like *Jeffery Combs*, at work. I am thankful for, and appreciate of all the experiences in my life that have brought me to this point. These experiences have all served as an education for where I am now. I pray that this work go on long after I have gone to that great beyond, where I will continue to expand and to assist others in doing the same. I pray that well being, love, peace, abundance, and happiness be yours all the days of your life, and that you radiate with the success and prosperity that you deserve and that I have allowed to flow within me.

For more on appreciation and gratitude, visit www.esteemnow.com

Contents

Introduction

Some Opening Words

"There is something new under the sun! Every stroke of my keyboard or yours, every breath you take, every song you sing, or race you run, or book you write, has newness in it! The world has never seen anything like your artistry in any calling. There will never be another like you, and none can duplicate your swing of the bat! Therefore, whatever you do is new. There Is Something New Under The Sun!"

__________*Tamir Qadree*

This is a book that is written for those who yearn for freedom from self-destruction and to have maximum self expression; for people from every walk of life. In writing this material, everyone is in mind in a literal sense. This is a book about you and every human being that has ever lived and that will ever live. This book is about us! This book is about *self-esteem, self reliance, self motivation, business* and the important factor that these play in our lives. The last few sentences might seem bold and over zealous to some of you, however, I offer as proof the fact/premise that, "Every human being yearns to feel important, and to have a healthy dose of self-esteem." While at times (it) this book may seem to be an auto-biography (about the author), it also is a biography of every reader. It is about going, *"Beyond Your Vision,"* and ultimately leaving a legacy of achievement for future generations. Somewhere on some page, and in some section or chapter, there will be a message that will be speaking directly to you; It is up to you to recognize it, ponder it, accept or reject and act or not act upon it. Once you recognize it and decide to act upon it, you will have opened the box to your, "ONE MINUTE TO HEALTHY ESTEEM."

Life is one big classroom and no one will ever force you to participate in the lessons that will guide you to a better, more rewarding life; the life that you truly desire. Success is voluntary, and no one will ever force it upon you. Successful is the one who finds and lives his or her true life calling or true self. When you find your true life calling, or true self, your mind will take you where you need to go. On the other hand, the life that the majority of the people live needs no urging on either. Simply said, people who have *low or no self-esteem*, will find anyway to *self-destruct* or remain, at best, in the same position in their life and in their soul. I am not only qualified to write to you about *self-esteem* and a number of related topics, I am your brother in humanity and life lessons. I have found that people all around us suffer from *low self-esteem, no self-esteem, warped self-esteem and inflated self-esteem.* The sad part about it is, *"self-esteem"*, is a word that I rarely, if ever, hear discussed. People just walk around wearing masks trying to hide deep and crusted issues that are literally destroying their lives. I see so many people masked with their heads hanging down, frowns on their faces, clothing dirty and cars filthy. These same people are just, "ONE MINUTE TO HEALTHY ESTEEM!" All they need is a wake up call; the Reclining Master Will Awaken! Have you ever gotten into a car and the driver apologizes for the way his car looks? Have you ever visited someone and asked to use the restroom only to be told, "Just one minute let me make sure everything is alright?" Have you ever complimented someone on their talents only to have them reply, "I am alright, but nothing big." Have you ever had anyone ask you, "Do you think that I can get the job?" Have you ever gone to someone's home and did not want to sit, and definitely did not want to drink water or eat anything? Have you ever had someone say to you, "I need to get my life on track." Have you ever smiled at someone and they turned their head or stared as if you just perpetrated a crime? All of these are often indicators of low *self-esteem* on some level or another. I am not saying that that is the only issue or that that is always the case. (I am not attempting to suggest that each indicator is indicative of an issue with self esteem.) However, I feel comfortable in saying, *"I believe that most of the problems involving the masses and even the classes, are tied to this thing we call self-esteem."* Having healthy *self-esteem* is like having fresh air or a drink of cool water on a hot sunny day. *Self-esteem* is the building block for *self-confidence, self-reliance, self-direction, self-motivation, and self-control.* It is (my) the writer's feeling that *self-esteem* is the *soul's palace!* In this *palace* lies all the knowledge that reminds us of what we truly are, and of the greatness in all of us. This greatness is waiting to be expressed for the benefit of the whole world. I speak from experience, and nearly 40 years of trials and tribulation that lead me to this conclusion. I believe that once you read this book and ponder the analogies, stories and anecdotes, you will discover your, "ONE MINUTE TO HEALTHY ESTEEM." When you are ready to stop fighting, denying and blaming others, when you are ready to take off that ego, you will find that the there is only a thin line that separate low self esteem from healthy self esteem. I KNOW that all there is, is ONE MINUTE TO HEALTHY ESTEEM."

This book is for all those who have come to the realization that they are ready and committed to making the change that will impact their development and positive self-direction. This book is not about theory or flowery language. If you are looking for anything other than a strong remedy (medicine) for effecting a positive difference in your life, (development and positive *self-direction)* then, this is not the book. Let's get into our imagination and *beyond our visions!* This is a time to put off your ego and let your heart and mind do their work for you! This is a time to be open and more honest with *yourself* than you have ever been before. No one is going to care about the fact that you are an under or over achiever, or a drunk or a violent angry person, until you do. No one can change you and no one will spend their valuable time trying because, you are valuable also. You are not a baby! Forget about what happened when you were a child; quit blaming your parents, sister, brother or whomever for your issues, if this is what you do. Grow up and be responsible, if you are not being responsible! Stop lying (if you are) to yourself and others, knowing full well that many of you are scared of the *dark,* scared of *success and failure*, scared of being looked in the *eye* and scared to *die!* Many of you are afraid of many things so, "admit it to yourself!" Admit that you have been afraid, but not any more! Say it, just like that, and feel good about your self now and always. You Are, "ONE MINUTE TO HEALTHY ESTEEM!"

You can't fool me, you can't fool the guy down the street, you cannot even fool you! We see you as you are! Free you from yourself, and come clean with yourself. Nobody wants to hear your sob story as we all have sob stories of our own, and they don't sell well, except to people that are as weak as the one telling it. Sob stories are for those wishing to develop a "sob" support group featuring the storyteller as, *"the chief whiner."* How long are you going to deceive yourself and attempt to setup others to fall for your sympathy pleas? When was the last time you invited someone over to your place of residence, (*if you have one)* and felt comfortable, without feeling the need to apologize for the house being untidy? I have been in a situation where I did not have a place of residence; I slept under park benches and so on. I have earned the right to speak to you like this. When was the last time you withheld information (if this applies to you) on an application for employment or credit? Yet you exclaim, *"no one will hire me or give me credit!"* I wonder why! Do you wonder why, or do you know as I do, that, *"you are getting all you are asking for and worth!"* You are right if you are thinking that you are worth more; no one cares if you don't live it and act like it. I will tell you that, "the moment you build your *self-esteem,* things will change for you. I can promise you this, *"if you take the stories, anecdotes, and suggestions in this book and use them with sincerity of purpose, your life will transform with blinding speed.* How do I know? When you have a healthy self-esteem, you call your own plays/shots! I am speaking from first hand experience, not theory and I did not feel a need or desire to seek a *"Grand Pooh-Bah"* to sanction what I am writing. You will not need anyone to confirm or deny that your life has changed in a dramatic way; money and things have nothing to do with it; they are the effect of a cause that is inner. You see, people can give you a reputation, but only you can build your character. When you have character (as we will discuss in a later chapter) you have personal magnetism and an attractive personality, you need no approval to get it. I do not care if you are a drunk, a criminal, the president of a fortune 500 company or a college student. I do not care if you are in sales, network marketing sales or retail sales, or just a house mom or dad. You can be an engineer, a marine biologist, a nurse, a gardener, or an astronaut, it truly does not matter. I do not care if you are a fifty year sales professional, a great motivational speaker and trainer, a world renowned actor, musician, the king of anywhere, or the top man on mars. I do not care if you are a billionaire or a millionaire with one hundred houses, fifty wives and you could own half of the globe! If you breathe, eat and sleep, if you are a human being with self-esteem issues, the message in THIS BOOK will serve you well. If you have a healthy dose of *self-esteem*, the message can only reinforce it, if you have a half tank of *self-esteem* the message can fill it up, if you have low or no self-esteem, the message can guide you to the attainment of what you need, by guiding you to "ONE MINUTE TO HEALTHY ESTEEM." There is one catch and that is this, "*It is all up to you and no one else!*" Your mind, with your desire and quick decision to build and maintain your healthy self-esteem, is vital to the way you feel about yourself and the way you see the world in which we live. This is your world, however, remember this, "*The world and the universe are all a bigger matter than you are!*" Be balanced and stay clear of overindulgence in self-importance. Your thoughts, dreams, goals and aspirations are what they are, but they are a miniscule part, if that, of the whole. You are only ONE MINUTE TO HEALTHY ESTEEM, so take the plunge and live life with joy.

USE THE MATERIAL; STAY WITH IT AND, YOU WILL ADVANCE BEYOND YOUR DEEPEST DESIRES; I GUARANTEE THIS! YOUR SOUL WILL DANCE AND YOUR HEART WILL BECOME LIGHT; YOU WILL FIND PEACE OF MIND. YOU WILL FIND JOY AND BE HAPPY! HAPPINESS IS BEYOND PEACE OF MIND AND ONCE YOU FIND THESE (INSIDE OF YOU) YOUR WORLD WILL BE BRIGHTER AND THE RAIN WILL WASH AWAY ALL THE STAINS OF YESTERDAY.

Master Awaken! Awaken All the Days of Your Life

Tamir Qadree
(With Gary)
April 20, 2005
www.esteemnow.com

Master

The Master reclines in the calm;
In the core of me. Master, guide me
Abide in me and lead me on.

The Master leads me through the night;
Showing me a shinning star, so bright.
Master rises with the peace, from the east,
Setting in the west and teaching the best.

The Master and the student are the same,
When the Master appeared, the student came.
The Master soothes the beast, and the burdens
Are no more.

The silence that creates makes the flowers bloom.
The Master calculates and grooms.
The character will publish the Master's plan;
Will you understand? You are but a grain of sand,
In the grand plan. In you the Master Stands!

The Master will guide you and make you feel
Satisfied. Do you need a guide; because in you,
The Master resides!

Master awakens, to peace, love and happiness;
Master, bless the child that lives in us all!
The Master holds the key to our life's call.

The Master Awakens

Chapter 1 The Master Awakened!

Master told me one day, I'd find peace in every way, but in search for the clues, wrong things I was bound to do, and he said, "Keep Your Head to the Sky." Keep Your Head to The Sky. Gave me the will to be free, purpose to live, is reality. When I found myself, never alone, changes came to make me strong. Step right up and be a man, you'll need faith to understand, because I was just saying for you to hear, "Keep Your Head In faith Atmosphere; Keep Your Head to The Sky."

I was thirteen years old when I heard those beautiful, soul-searching lyrics. They were music to my soul and harmony to my total being, in a world of chaos, bullying and death. I would listen to those lyrics over and over again until I asked, "*Who is The Master?*" Then, shortly after that song, the same group, *Earth, Wind & Fire* released what would be another message to my soul and illuminate my being; the song was titled, *"Devotion."* "*Through devotion, blessed are the children, praise the teacher, that brings true love to many, your devotion opens all life treasures; and deliverance from the fruits of evil.*" These songs stirred something deep in me, my yearning gave me strength; most of all they gave me belief, but beyond belief, I had a certain *knowingness* that I did not understand. there was comfort in those lyrics from the bullying, denying, self hating environment of the hell hole that I had lived in. I was hemmed in by our crowded two bedroom apartment with eleven children and two adults until my mother and father separated. I was searching for the peace that *Earth, Wind & Fire* sang about. I knew that they were speaking directly to me. My soul connected with that of *Maurice White's* wisdom, the sheen of *Phillip Bailey's* voice, the depth of *Verdine White's* bass guitar, with the exceptional percussions and background vocals of *Ralph Johnson*; and with the masterfully composed symphony of the band, the majestic sound of the horns and the heavenly, angelic, ringing voices. I felt the foundation of the Earth beneath my feet, the Wind of life in my spirit; these combined, created *The Fires of Desire In My Soul!* They were the *Mighty Elements* that were creating who I am today; they laid the foundation of the realization that my Head is in Heaven and my feet on the earth; with that knowledge, I am lead to you, as you read these words.

Who is The Master?

I did not know; I was too busy running from bullies that were kicking my butt and assaulting me at school, at play and in the dark. I had to be big, think big, look, act and talk big, laugh big, and get a big approval from everyone; when I did not, I would create something, even if it meant telling a lie to get it. I was always center stage in school, always the first to raise my hand and speak the loudest. I was a class bully, and that is exactly what happened to me over the next 40 years of my life. I attracted just what I became! I attracted anger, lies deceit, and broken promises and missed opportunities. I would bury myself in a false sense of self. I had no real value; at least, *I did not believe that I did.* I had only fake value. I was searching for The Master and the clue, and wrong things I did do. I would repent only to repeat the offense like some junky, up and down an emotional and moral roller coaster. I could not rest, and rarely told anyone my transgressions. I prided myself on being open with my faults; however, I was shielding the deeper and the most damaging faults. My language was harsh, abusive and cutting towards others. I did not understand nor did I want to hear things that did not agree with my false self, my ego self. I was actually shielding my ego, by admitting certain things while hiding the true causes. I was admitting the effects without dealing with the *cause* within. I have gone on to learn that many people lead such lives, pretentiously existing and calling it, "*living life.*" I would feel embarrassed whenever I thought about those days filled with masquerading characters, phony shows of courage, intelligence and overly indulged self importance. I could now imagine that there were onlookers who saw me for just the character I was; I was hiding and pretending, but the people with peace in their hearts saw me. I was a walking bundle of nervous energy, scared, broke, busted and disgusted with my life. I talked a good game, however, life did not reflect the game that I spoke, my home life did not reflect the love that I pretended to know, my business life did not measure up and others that saw me from a distant would ask, *"Why?"*

The Abused Becomes the Abusive

I knew long before I became an adult that I had the gift of speech that could cause you to love me dearly or to hate me clearly, and despise me for the rest of your life. I was that good at hurting people or that endearing to others, making friends, admirers or enemies for life. I was a master of the "destructive, human will-breaking, *word*." Those words were me and I were them, but little did I know, "I was destroying myself." Although I was capable of some of the most beautiful writings, my letters were often the rebuking, cutting, demeaning type. If you got in my world, (*my ego world)* I would write a letter and believe me, few people cared to spar with me in the arena. They could not handle it; I became worse and meaner. My life was a series of high energy moments, mixed with violent energy that others could not deal with. I called it "*The Fire."* I prided myself on my fiery speech, demeanor and drive. That was the same fire of my enemy, *"my would-be assassin*" within. He was surely "*inside"* to get me, but, there is *The Master* in me; he promised that I would find peace in every way; I listened to this voice inside of me that comforted me, but when the immediate danger or distress was over, I would go back and drink from the same destructive fountain.

I had been bullied all my life. I was scared and trembling in dark rooms, and I was told that the demons would get me if I did not behave, The *Wolf Man* in particular! The demons (*in my own mind,)* created from someone else and given, have visited me at will since I was a 5 year old child or perhaps younger; they tortured and taunted, teased, humiliated and raped me of my peace of mind. They were of my own mind, my own creation. Since I was a little boy named *Gary,* I was attacked; I was innocent and did not (consciously) ask for this curse upon my inner being. The Master promises to protect his little ones. The Deliverer would come and rescue *Gary* from the keep of the *Whisperer or Chatterer which* had long lodged in my mind. The deliverer had to be someone strong, well read and verse in affirmations of a strongly positive nature. This take over was approximately 14 to 15 years old before the little boy, *Gary,* chose a helper. Then it would take another 25 years before the deliverance. Hell is no peace! Peace is no hell; you can have it anyway you desire, and all you have to do is decide. *Gary* did not decide his fate; how can anyone blame a child less than 6 years of age. However, *The Master* gave me so much value and ability, that *Gary* had to grow enough to gain the strength; the will to live, to choose and fight and be victorious.

"Gave me the will to be free, purpose to live is reality. When I found myself never alone, changes came to make me strong."

The Manipulators

The bully would get me to manipulate everything for his own good and no one else. He was bigger than me and he knew how to threaten me to get me to do what he wanted. Even though I had ten sisters and brothers, I was too frightened to tell them that the bully would hurt me if I expose him. He was so abusive at school, in the playground in the streets that I could never get him to get out of my life. I started my bulling tactic on the girl upstairs; I would always take her money and push her around like the neighborhood bully would do me. When I would get in trouble in school, I would accuse the teacher of not liking me because I was small for my age. It worked like a charm, so I decided to make it a life long pattern of abuse and manipulate things that served me, and things that I could share to please my bully friend. It became a nasty, insane habit. After all, I was taught by the best bully in the city, and I heard since then that they have gotten better at it, but only now he works the adult circuit and have connections in every part of the world. I was abused at an early age, but, *"The Abused Had Become the Abusive."* I was still in search of "*The Master.*" I did not find peace from the bully. I found abuse and sarcasm, taunting and ridicule. I stole from the grocery store to prove my courage and to feed the bully. My self-esteem has suffered for years. I sought approval desperately. I wanted to prove my heart and daring, all the while, I was proving my self hatred and disdain for success in life. Funny how it works and how it keeps working until we take upon ourselves the responsibility for change by changing our minds and coming into our peace, which is our sheer power!

Closing Doors and Turning off the lights

Teddy Pendegrass put out love songs titled, *"Turn Out The Lights and Close The Door;"* He was wasting his precious breath by telling me that! Even though it was a love song, I was not turning off any lights and I sure as hell was not closing any doors. I was scared to death! Of what?

All of my child life and ninety nine percent of my adult life, I had been locking doors, closing curtains and turning off lights at night. I would say to anyone who would listen, *"when it is dark, people can see in your house, but you cannot see them because you are in the light."* I would say, *"It is dangerous out there."* I knew that someone, or some burglar or murderer could find easy victims. I was ready and would always protect my family. I was attracting what I sought to avoid. No one was coming, because the thing that I feared was already in! I saw him every time I looked into the mirror. I felt him every time I exploded with anger or wrote someone a nasty letter. I smelt him when his ego and pride were wounded as he ran to seek approval from "well meaning" friends who *fed the Beast,* dressed his wounds and gave him license to do it again. This went on repeatedly for 40 years. Like salt and pepper, like the beauty and the beast, "I lived two lives and one was always dominating the other. I kept up this pattern of self abuse by abusing others, *(The Beast)* then feeling sorry *(The Beauty)* and often apologizing. I would get hurt and feel down and would seek validation about my *fiery words* and how blessed I was. At other times

I would do and say things that only angels could do and bring light to an entire room just by entering *(The Beauty)* then, after hearing or seeing something which I did not agree with, I would explode or cut with words (The Beast) that were usually overly expressed; they were aimed to inflict pain. The truth is that I was addicted to pain and temporary relief which came from my sympathizers. I would keep this abusive, mentally unstable condition for nearly 40 years.

I was vigilant every night about all the doors and windows being locked. If I found one unlocked, I would say to my wife and children, *"you guys are just loose and silly, don't you know that you are supposed to lock doors?"* I am from Chicago, and we know better, someone could come in and kill you. Because of my fears and belief that the bully would get me in the dark, like he had done all my life, I would turn on the front bathroom light so that when my children get up in the middle of the night to get into bed with their mom and me, they would discover that the lights were left on. I was living my fears through my children, but, worse yet, *"I was passing my fears on to my children!"* I no longer do this, thanks to the light that now shines in my heart and soul. The light of understanding and hope is one of the beautiful jewels of wisdom. I now pass on this light to my children, and teach them that they must learn to *"see in the dark."* Mastery over the dark is mastery of our fears, doubts, worries and all the destructive forces that have built up mental prisons in many people.

When I sat in my office, I would make sure that the curtain was closed to the point where no one could see in, after all, "it was often early in the morning, because I had the habit of praying before the birds got up." Predators could look in, in fact, I knew someone could climb over my fence and look at me while I was praying or doing my reading. One day my wife said, "Tamir, I notice that you always have this curtain totally closed, why? Are you afraid that someone could see you?" I said, *"That is crazy, I just close the curtains, because I am comfortable, we all have our own comfort zone."* The window represented the window to my soul and I could not face my self, I was afraid of what I would see. I knew that I would see the *Wolf Man!* I did not know it on a conscious level as plainly as I did on a subconscious level. The fear had seized my mind at an early age and I did not understand it or understand the need to release myself from the captivity. I was being purged and prepared for something great, to serve humanity; for what or in what exact way, I did not know.

"A Careful inventory of all your past experiences may disclose the startling fact that everything has happened for the best." Unknown

Chapter 2 The Wolf Man

(The Coward Bully Within)

When I was a little boy, I watched a movie called, "The *Wolf Man"* starring an old actor named, "Lon Chaney". The Wolf Man would turn into a mad animal on two feet when the moon came out. Being bitten by a wolf brought about this cursed condition. There was a gypsy woman who knew who *The Wolf Man* was, and who also knew that he was suffering. One day, while attacking or attempting to attack a lady, who was his girl friend, he was maimed and his mask came off. He was finally at peace; his wounds were fatal. I was allowed to watch this movie several times as a child. I was called *"The Wolf Man"* and *"Hairy faced Gary"* when I was a little boy, because of my hairy little face and body. *"I had been bitten by the Wolf!"* I was allowed to watch this madness as a 4-5 year old child. I had nightmares and was terrified of the *"Wolf Man."* I became the *"Wolf Man."* I ran just like he did, "from the darkness." I ran for about 40 years of my life. I never stopped running and blaming others, being paranoid about things and people conspiring against me. I was a nervous wreck. I would chew my finger nails to the quick, until they bled. Then, I would start on the skin around my finger nails. I was a compulsive nail bitter and I did not know how to stop the habit. I managed to stop temporarily on two or three occasions, but I would always bite them eventually. I had gotten used to the taste of blood from my fingers. I would run down the alley in Chicago bare feet when I was about four and five years old, just like the character did in the Wolf

Man movie. I would wake up and my mother and siblings would tell me what I had done, just like the character in the movie. This was around the time I believe that I first saw the movie, which further cemented what I had become. I feared going to sleep, just like the character in the movie.

I was suffering and it was through no fault of my own; I had suffered from a disease called, *"Lycanthropy," which is defined as; 1. A delusion that, one has become a wolf. 2. The assumption of the form and characteristics of a wolf held to be possible by witchcraft or magic.* Words have a magical and can even have a diabolical affect on the mind, especially young tender minds of little children. When I was around thirteen years old, I took to the streets one day and confronted a boy much bigger than I was. I thought I was *Bruce Lee* and, he knocked my two front teeth out, proving that I was not the famous man of martial arts! They (my two front teeth) were swimming around in my mouth like dead fish. I had fangs like a wolf now. It was what I wanted *psychologically /subconsciously*, and I created it! My upper front teeth were out, and the two sharper ones on the side were like fangs! My subconscious mind had been impressed with the images on the screen and the names "*Wally wolf and hairy face Gary,*" that I had been called all of my life by my siblings.

"We Become What We Think About." I had become what I feared," The Wolf Man". Believe me, the thought haunted me. The more I ran, the faster, harder and more determined it was to catch, keep and

ultimately kill me. It was catching me and I was running out of places to run to!

When I was growing up in those years in the streets of Chicago, fighting was a mark of your manhood or a tough man thing. Many of us worshiped guys that were good with their hands and feet. We talked about fighting and learned how to fight. It was the way it was and the way of the concrete jungle in the sixties and seventies. I had a reputation for biting my opponents when I fought, *(Like the Wolf Man)* who were usually hand picked by me. I won about ninety five percent of all my fights, however, the other five percent were not scared by my bluff, nor were they impressed by my fangs and fuming like an animal; "they wanted to extract a few more teeth, but, I was not having that!" The weak thought that I was crazy and they would say, *"He is the craziest one in that family and he will hurt someone."* They were feeding my already murdered *self-esteem* and validating my cowardly actions. I would get into street fights with people, and sometimes, I would show my fangs and widen my eyes. One hundred percent of the time, my opponents would back away thinking that I was crazy or mad. I doubt if anyone of them were in their peace, because if they were, they would have noticed my bluff and seen me for the coward I was. I was mean and had a violent, soul stirring temper with which. I stirred my own soul everyday. Does any of this surprise you? After all, I was living out the character in the movie, the character that had frightened the little boy in me. I had not only feared him, I had *become* him in every way."

The Wolf Man had no peace and as already mentioned; he died in the movie. I told my sister in early 2004 that I knew how I was supposed to die! I had made statements like that several times since I was 22 years of age. I told her that I would be "*shot*" for speaking out against worldly injustice and that it was my destiny. What I was doing was setting myself up to quit and take the coward's way out of my pain and life long suffering. I had no peace and my nerves would drive me to near insanity. I wanted to be this person or that person; I had a martyr complex and was subconsciously committing suicide. My true motive was brilliantly disguised to those who themselves were imprisoned by their own inner turmoil. But, those who could see the light, probably understood, and that part causes me to laugh at myself when I think about it.

My Ailing Self-Esteem

I would drive and fantasize about being this person or that person, especially athletes, singers and great speakers. This was no normal admiration, nor was it healthy! I would be day dreaming and someone would say, *"Hello, are you there?"* I would get upset if anyone would disturb my fantasy world. I did this up until my day of deliverance from the bullying, lying Whisperer / Chatterer, who had robbed a very young boy of his natural joy. I would actually get in these zones. The real sad part was that I thought that it was alright to have fantasies like that. I had totally buried my sense of self-worth and saw greatness lived through someone else's achievements. I had neither the courage nor the decisiveness to accomplish great feats because I did not value myself. This was all subconscious destruction, because consciously, I thought I was the man. Success to me was proving what I can do *"then I will show them."* I always wanted to show someone else how smart, fabulous and intelligent I was. Then those enablers would stroke my wounded *self-esteem* by saying *"you are great and dynamic."* That kept me doing fake deeds, living in a dream world; then I would get some more compliments, only to repeat the sad process for life. Finally I was beginning to get so desperate, because I felt that time was running out and I didn't have the material things nor the recognition that I sought outside, all the while not seeing that I was all that I needed, because, *"God had made me the most precious thing ever created."* I would learn that *"things,"* do not bring happiness! *Happiness brings happiness and being in the process brings happiness and success.* Success is not a life that is free of adversity and trials; success is a life of all those things, until those things are put behind and overcome. Thus, the secret to success is learning to be, do and have, despite the circumstances, which will eventually create new and more desirable circumstances. Successful people go through and have gone through much of the same things that unsuccessful people go through, but they go through with more dignity and assurance, therefore they persevere and keep their eyes on their prize and they succeed! At that point, others will say, "so and so is a great success and how fortunate he or she is."

Finally "The Deliverance"

When I was 12, my aunt's husband would call me over to hear me speak of my vision and dream for world peace and harmony. I would give speeches for him and his drinking buddies. My talks were about life, living joyously, happy and loving all the world over. I did not know where this information was coming from, but I felt an affinity with my visions of world love, peace, harmony and prosperity. My aunt's husband would tell everyone how intelligent I was to be so young, and that everyone should listen in. They would gather around and I would go; my talks were never rehearsed nor planned, I just let got and magic came out. *Gary* was speaking from within me, while being imprisoned by the Whisperer and told, "If you attempt to escape, the *Wolf Man* will get you." I went to California in October, 1974, the year after I heard the master speak to me. I heard another song called devotion. It said, *"Through devotion, blessed are the children, praise the teacher, who brings true love to many, your devotion, opens all life treasures; and deliverance from the fruits of evil.*

When I was 19 years old, I was heart broken over a love affair. My girl friend slept with one of the guys in the neighborhood in my apartment, in my bed, eating my cereal and wearing my bathrobe, listening to my music, and just maybe they had sex! Hummmmmm........... I did not deal with it well. I attempted to accept it, but it was hard. I start having great thoughts of violence, revenge and I did not want to confront the guy, as that would show weakness, especially if I could not beat him up; I did approach him eventually, in a very low key way. I felt devastated because everyone in the neighborhood knew it. My *self-esteem* had taken a deep emotional blow. This time I was really out of control. I was hurt and mad as hell and I had every right to be! My girl friend moved out and she said, "You are a monster!" I could not sleep, I was afraid of the dark and I knew that the *Wolf Man* was in me. I would get up at night and look for mischief in the neighborhood, with my sister's boyfriend. One day, my ex-girl friend came to my house to get her things and she brought her new boy friend over; I gave her the things and she left. I was torn apart and really down. I thought about getting a pistol and setting things right. She had confronted me with a bigger man and I had to prove my self-value by standing up and confronting her in return. One day, I ran face to face with the young man whom she had brought to my house and he said, "Don't approach my girl friend no more." The next night, my friend and I went out to do something. We went riding around looking for trouble; we met a young man who was selling marijuana. I shot him in the leg over a dispute about the transaction. The next day, I observed a policeman looking into my car, so I came out of my mother's apartment and asked, "Why are you looking in my car?" 10 minutes later I was arrested, and eventually sentenced to serve time in the California Penal System. I was a wild animal caged and for good reason. My self-esteem had taken such a beating I had to have relief. That relief of being locked up saved me from destroying the rest of my life. I could not figure out what happened, then one day during the summer of 1981 in the month of Ramadan, which means; *a burning of the old self to bring out the new, renewed life, or that original nature founded on peace and bliss.* I changed my name to *Tamir (fruitful and prosperous) Muhammad (The one who praised God) Qadree (My Might, Strength)* Gary had chosen that name. Gary was still a little boy who had never had a chance to find peace from the *Wolf Man* movies that he had seen and that he had become. He knew it, but not consciously. Gary (I was told) means "strong" and the last name Qadree, means "my might, strength." Gary was making preparations for the big push for the liberation of his soul from the *Whisperer* who had stolen his bliss at the ripe age of 5 years old or younger. 14 years had past since Gary had been bullied, and Whispered to by the coward. 14 years had past since being put in dark closets and told horror stories by his siblings. 14 years of being called "The Wolf Man."

The Master had told me that he would find peace one day, but in search for the clue, wrong things I was bound to do! That is what the Master told me. After 4 years and 7 months I was released only to find that my problems were just beginning. For the next 21 years, I would run and suffer great mental and taunting anguish. People would hear me speak or perform some service and would say, "Dude, you should be on Oprah or something." While I loved the compliment, it was a hard blow against my self-esteem once again. Everywhere I went I could not avoid being noticed and singled out for greatness, however, I never knew that we all have it right now within us. *Gary* was pushing *Tamir* to free him. *Tamir* was dragging and pushing to "prove his worth," instead of being worthy and chosen by *Gary* to perform the huge task ahead, and that was the claiming of the self-esteem that the little boy *(Gary)* deserved to come into. *Gary* had stayed alive. Imagine a 5 year old boy (or younger) never growing up being trapped in his own body, being bullied by nothingness, wretched coward called "*The Whisperer.*" *Gary* had the courage, *Tamir* had the knowledge, the adult experience to read, study, go to seminars and read all the self-help books; *Muhammad* knew the purpose and that the purpose was to be worthy of praise and love, and *Qadree* was the self-control which was the strength. Fearing success, *Tamir* would always find a way to quit something no matter how genuine it was. *Tamir* would always self-destruct. *Gary* did not give up and neither did *Tamir; Tamir* would muster the courage from within and each time he got closer and closer, but together they would not be denied. Singly they were vulnerable, but as one, they would prove formidable for the *Whisperer,* and his cowardly *Wolf Man!* They would later drive him back to his emptiness.

In 1986 I lived in San Diego California. I moved there because my life was not on track and I had just had some terrible experiences emotionally from a broken engagement, which I believe was because of another man. This was an obvious blow to my wobbling, shaky *self-esteem*. I left San Jose, California in search of myself. I found a place to stay, after sleeping outside for about a week. People came to assist me and even help me with food and work. I worked two jobs and went to a night class. Then I decided that I would pursue my boxing career. I was a talented and promising young prospect for the ring and I knew it. I had some experience, but not a lot. I went to the gym in San Diego and met a man named, "Buddy." He was a strange man in that he was very secretive, but he always liked me and would help me. He taught me how to move and utilize my skill and talents, he named me, *"Tragic Magic,"* and people in the gym would marvel at the things and tools that I had as a fighter with very little actual ring experience. That name was actually describing what my life had been like. I was magic and tragic to my own success for many years before and many more to come. I sparred with his nephew who was a champion. This young man named Darryl was only fourteen years old, with about ninety amateur bouts and could whip a twenty five year old man. He fought like Muhammad Ali or Sugar Ray Leonard. This young man made me look bad, but then I began to take on his characteristics and after weeks of being humiliated by a fourteen year old boy, I calmed down and began to dish it out and take over. I recall one of his friends telling me this, *"he does not want to spar with you today because he knows that you are going to beat him up."* The student became the teacher! After a while people could not tell the difference between me and the child prodigy. I became the marvel of the gym. I was fast, strong, flashy, bold, daring and talkative, but I was timid, scared and nervous. My first pro fight was in Reseda California, where I met Michael Nunn, Terry Norris, Mike Weaver, and singer, Barry White, along with many other former and some then current champions. I wanted to be like them and knew that I could. It was August 26, 1996, and while I waited for my time to leave my dressing room, I prayed and then the knock came on my door. I ran to the ring, dancing and prancing like some prize stallion, with "tragic magic" written on my robe. When we were introduced I walked up to my opponent with the tenacity of a bulldog, the referee had to warn me for getting in the guys face and touching his nose with mine. When the bell rang, I ran out and hesitated! I was lost from that point on! I could here the crowd cheering me on saying, "Ali!" I remember scoring at will and doing some breath taking moves. It was going to be a wipe out in the first round! I continued on through the second round but with more anxiety; my mind was telling me to fall down, and quit as soon as he hits me. I was winning and looking good, but I did not want the victory, and my first signs of fearing success showed. I went to my corner for the third round to start and I told my trainer, "Buddy, I broke my hand!" Buddy then motioned to stop the fight. It was over and I had them put a wrapping on it. I knew that I had given up on my chance and later I was approached by many people in the boxing circle in L.A. and San Diego about my skills and ability. They did not see the "fear of success." Most people do not understand it, most of them did not. I thought that I was a coward for quitting and the rest. I have lived with that secret for 17 years, but it was no secret at all. “I knew it.” *That is all that would really count in the game of life.*

The Wolf Man was afraid of himself, so was I. “I had become him since I was 5 years old or younger. There can be no success when you fear who you are. You are the only one that can guarantee your success. Success is a journey and not some destination. I too, feared what it would be like to be truly me. I was so cloaked with masks and facades; I had forgotten, and did not respect who or what I really was. “I am a valuable, precious human being, and I need approval from no one for anything that I do.” The Master told me so. I am the master!

Opportunities

In the work force, I have had some of the most promising positions that an inner city boy from the ghetto could get. Yet, sure enough as I would get in the best or greatest position to excel and move up, something would happen. Because I was black, (so I thought) white corporate America could not seem to cope with a successful black man. They were always jealous and trying to hold me back because I was a threat to them. Most blacks and many whites agreed with me, but I definitely played my part in most of the incidences, not making things any easier to resolve. I have filed federal complaints about 6 times and have been involved in 2 law suits. Each time the battle was brutal and draining on my spirit. I vowed to never let anything in life hold me back. Corporate America could not stand to see a young black man rise, yet they would always hire me, pay me good, brag about me, then suddenly for no apparent reason, they would turn on me, time and time again. Every six months or so, my wife would be worried that I had blown a great opportunity. I always made her a prophet. I did not want success, I only wanted to bluff and growl and bite people who were weak and willing victims. I thought I wanted success, but I wanted peace from my pain and the *Whisperer* had a remedy. I was killing my opportunities and creating excuses to burn all bridges. *"I would later come to realize that all things work together for a destined purpose, namely that, I was being prepared for something greater and much more dynamic than working a regular job."* I was terminally unemployable. My good friend calls it, *"psychologically unemployable."* I could not, by choice, handle the thought that I would be bound into someone else's dream, with them dictating the pace of my life, then, retire with all of my dreams unfulfilled. I had no peace. I could not sleep a whole night and sought to prove and display my value in ways that were demeaning to others. I would talk about myself, in order to feel higher than the person that I was speaking with; especially when I knew that they did not have a clue as to their life mission. I felt big, yet I was hurting and the pain was taking its toll on my ailing *self-esteem.* When you can face another human being and see their lack of ambition, and talk about yours, you are saying, *"I am somebody," in* essence you are saying, *"I have something going and you don't."* That is bullying. I played the bully hundreds of times in my life. I have learned that, in order to see beauty in others, you have to make some beauty and see it in others. We all have the seed of beauty and greatness in us; the enlightened ones (people) will see it and smile at it; the hurting, bullying, self-destructing ones (people) will choke it and call it mean names.

When I would run while training for boxing or just for health, I would run with my head down and I would walk the same way. From this is where I get my most creative thoughts. Imagine this, *"getting my most creative thoughts with my head down!"* Creative thoughts and Head down is really a contradiction in terms. I would be in my comfort zone cruising along in my own world. My mother would walk with her head down and I would say, *"Pick your head up."* I knew in my subconscious mind that something was not right; however, I did not see my own issue. My head felt more comfortable being down because the muscles in the neck were weak and did not feel comfortable being *upright.* My mother looked like she was lost when she walked, because of the slump in her shoulders with her head always toward the ground. I did the exact same thing and must have looked the same way. When I noticed the way I walked, I made a conscious effort to walk upright. It hurt, and was tiresome for my neck for a little while, but the muscle got stronger and stronger and I felt natural and better inside also. I was so accustomed to walking with my head down because my *self-esteem* was beaten. Now, my head goes up automatically. If I were to put my head down without justification, The

Master within would say, *"Keep your head up."* Funny how that works! Your inner being is ready to serve you and direct you; you must be willing to allow it to do your bidding, by what you put in it.

The Master gave me the will to be free, purpose to live is reality, when I found myself never alone, changes came to make me strong. Step right up and be a man, you'll need faith to understand. I was just saying for you to hear, keep your head in faith atmosphere.

After many, many experiences over the next 17 years, the defining moments came at last! Funny how this works. I do, say and think things that could destroy me, yet some of those same words, inner voices and movies of greatness, *"served me in a positive way."* I did not know it, but I was tired, behind on my promises and my wife was emotionally baffled. She knew that I suffered but like the many priest and clergy, friends and acquaintances, she had no answers. The answer had to come from the blood brothers, *"Gary and Tamir."* They would later become what I call the "*Twin Masters*" of Their Own Destiny. They lived in *probable realities* that were different, yet they stayed connected in a most miraculous way. They were one, just like a coin with two sides; each watched the others back and stayed on guard.

The Turning Point

The turning point came on November 6, 2004 at the national convention sponsored by a company with which I was affiliated. It was a great event with Jeffery Combs as the guest speaker. Jeffery was good, natural and very intuitive. When I talked with him; he seemed to pierce my soul with every look. I felt uneasy at times, but I gathered myself and asked if he would consider endorsing my book. He asked if I would attend his "Breakthrough to Success" seminar. In response, I told him that I had to speak with my wife, yet when I walked away, I went nowhere near her. He seemed to observe my every move. I could feel him. Why was I ashamed to say that I did not have the money to attend? Why did I pretend and put on a mask, or why did I even have a mask to put on? Somehow, I knew that he knew, and I approached him and said, *"I don't have the money, but I will be there."* Later that night when we were receiving the awards and rings, (those who did) the moment of truth and *self-realization came.* I had received many accolades all weekend; I was a little god, a celebrity and a superstar among my business partners and my peers. I had blown everyone away as far as recruiting new business associates was concerned, and I had qualified for the ring before anyone else. I had made the double digit plaque, which listed the names of the business builders that recruited 10 or more in the month of June 2004. I recruited about 12 new associates. I was also the closest to earning my company car. Most of all I was the undisputed champ of the company in that I had received the coveted top award the past two times. 6 months earlier, 3 people had sworn to dethrone me and I had vowed to make them pay hell for the challenge! I surely did make them pay, as I was caught up in the politics, the hype and the emotion of the moment. I had actually forgotten, or lost sight of my own personal power and life's dreams in order to fit into someone else's dream. This, I have learned never to do again. Two of the people that had challenged me, never showed up to play during the summer, and the one who did, came no where close to defeating me for the coveted trophy. It was a lady from my home town, Chicago Illinois, who had dared to challenge my skill and my 18 months of dominance. *(These were my thoughts and attitudes and did not reflect her skills and the great person that she really is)* I got the top producer awards and was about to clean house, as I had done all weekend. I was a true celebrity in everyone's mind and especially my own. The president said, *"And now this award goes to a lady..."* There was a dead silence throughout the room, and everyone seemed to be in shock, especially me. I was not in shock, I was as mad as hell, and there would be an entire country to pay for such political games, slamming and chicanery. To add insult to injury, my business partner did not get her ring because of qualifications deadlines; we were not notified, which caused her deep hurt and embarrassment. She told her family members and friends, that she was going to get her ring. To add further insult to injury, she was forgotten on the next recognition also, however, after I reminded the president, they called her up and she wept like a little girl; I was infuriated and mad, *"like a*

Wolf." My pride was hurt and I felt that I had been disrespected in front of the whole country. After all, I was an important piece of the puzzle, and I was the big name. I hugged the victor and showed enough grace to leave after the dancing started. I later called the president to a private room, ripped him and gave the ring back, because he had just offended me, my team, and my family. I accused him of making a business move because people were tired of hearing my name called all of the time; (He often said that himself) I accused the president of playing on my competitive spirit, to make room for a company explosion in business. I would later accuse him and his business partner of creating a competition and then having the power to arbitrarily decide the winner. More importantly, it was that incident, on that weekend in November of 2004 that I would learn a lesson that is the most valuable in anyone's life! That lesson was this, "Never, never ever subordinate my life calling to fit into someone else's scheme!" That is sage advice for anyone, in any worthy calling in life; I learned that I could work with whomever I desired, however, if my life purpose is left out; I must stop and look at the total picture. I looked at myself, and what my life was at that point, stronger than I had been in years. I had gotten away from why I was doing the business and I had terribly forsaken my writing, speaking and coaching career; which really was why I was involved. That would change dramatically over the next six months.

For two months I fumed and fussed to anyone who would listen to my complaints. "It's not fair. They have robbed and snubbed me!" I ranted "After all that I have done for those guys and that company," I thought. I told him to go and find another poster boy. I was bitter, and thought that I had been betrayed. The *Whisperer* had been exposed. I did not know it at the moment, but I now believe that *Gary* did. The little boy knew it; he must have smiled; he would soon be free at last. No matter what the owners of the company did, my self-esteem was exposed for what it was, at that time in my life. I stopped to reflect that the company managers were who, and what they were, and had business motives. Later, I would learn to be gracious in temporary defeat and not to boast in victory, but savor victory and defeat as life's lesson and jewels. I learned to say, and embrace these words, "Nothing moves me!" I have since learned to be indifferent to failure or success, pain or pleasure. Whatever the universe, my higher self brings me is perfect, safe, friendly and for my highest good. I trust the universal goodness, the well being, and peace that it wants to flow powerfully through me always. I learned to detach, and leave the results and outcomes alone.

My pride was damaged, but my self-confidence was strong, so I decided to pull away from the owners of the company. I had been their spokesman in the field, their loyal friend. When California had taken a big hit with attrition, I was still standing and supporting the company. I had poured my heart and soul into the business, but they betrayed me, I believed, in front of the company that I was instrumental in building. I was the show and the main event. People came to hear

Tamir Qadree speak on Sunday conference calls. How dare they challenge my fame! They were surely and definitely out of their minds and were playing games with what I was on the road to accomplish. I wrote nasty letters, twice, and I made some people feel uneasy. I would never write letters like that today. I would never write a nasty letter to anyone for any reason.

I started my own conference calls that were paid for by eleven other people and me. I created a master mind group of individuals, most of whom would not enroll anyone, even if someone walked up to them and said, *"Sign me up!"* This was really a support group for my "*ego,"* or "*bruised self-esteem,* "and also people who worshiped and fed my monstrous ego. Fortunately, four members of the group were the real deal, and awesome entrepreneurs. About four months prior to the incident at the conference, I had started to read a book entitled, "*As A Man Thinketh."* I had previously read the book twenty years earlier. I read and re-read the book over and over again especially the last chapter on Serenity. I read serenity everyday for about fifty consecutive days after my humiliation at the conference. I sought peace and tranquility for my hurt and bruised ego. James Allen wrote, *"self-control is strength, right thought is mastery and calmness is power, say unto your heart peace be still"* These would be the words that would lead me back to the peace and tranquility that we are all born with; the peace that *Gary* was guiding me to. These words became my companion and a soothing balm when the pain was harder than I could stand. My soul received them and I was comforted. The words became flesh and they manifested in my personality.

Those words formed my being; grasped my soul and gave me comfort from my scorched and wounded ego. Over the next one hundred and five days. I wrote in all my affirmations, "*I am peace, I am sweet and I am serene.*" I repeated this over and over again. I carried cards that read the same and quoted several passages from the book. Little did I know that, "I had summoned a source of power that makes men and women great and powerful beyond imagination." My soul was stirring; my conscious mind was giving instructions to my subconscious mind. I was also instructing my sub-conscious mind with messages from such store houses of knowledge from books and people like, *"Think and Grow Rich, The Game of Life and How to Play it, How to Win Friends and Influence People, Emerson, Thoreau, Les Brown, Tony Robbins, Muhammad The Prophet, Emotional Intelligence, Self-Efficacy, Grow Rich with Peace of Mind, The Magic of Thinking Big, The Law of Success In Sixteen Lessons, The Holy Bible, The Holy Qur'an, Lead the Field and The Power Of Ambition Audio Programs,"* and many others enlightening sources of inspiration and hope. I searched far and wide as I had always done, yet this time was different. Being a great reader, I read many other books as well, but these I read everyday and some twice per day. I was searching for something, and I wanted to find it now, today. I was being tortured and I was about to ruin the relationship I had built with the company that I was working with. I had assisted in destroying every form of employment in the past because I was terminally unemployable; now I was destroying this one because of false pride, a damaged ego, and low self-esteem. I came to realize that my ego was always pushing me around and tricking me. I had lived in the ocean of adversity and turmoil for many years and it was taking its toll on my mind, my body and my spirit. I had learned from the late great, Dr. Norman Vincent Peale that, "Adversity is no bad thing; it doesn't feel good, but it is not bad."

Napoleon Hill wrote; *"Adversities and temporary defeat are generally blessings in disguise, for the reason that they force one to use both imagination and decision. This is why a man usually makes a better fight when his back is to the wall and he knows there is not retreat. He then reaches the decision to fight instead of running. The Imagination is never quite so active as it is when one faces some emergency calling for quick and definite decision and action."*

These setbacks or occurrences would take place my entire life; I knew that there was something deeper and more meaningful for me, and I was and am destined to find it. I decided to go for my dreams and aspirations! My life and my death would all symbolize my journey to my life calling and, I knew that I was close and in the process. I would not be denied and I shall not quit nor abandon my life mission; my mission is my life and to leave it and not to develop it would be tantamount to suicide. I may as well be dead in the flesh if my *perfect self expression* is not fed and nurtured. It is what the *Creator* gave me. Each of us has something that he or she is to do that no one else is to do in the same way. To search and thrive is the ideal, and no one will do it for us; in fact, "no one can do it for us!"

The greatest reverses and misfortunes of life often open the door
To golden opportunities."

The Reclining Master Awaken

Chapter 3 Peace in Every Way

The Master told me one day, that I would find peace in everyway. How does that Master, The Creator of all things, know all things? The Master is One, and all things are created from that One powerful source I refer to as *"Master,"* he resides in each and everything that was created; That is *"The Master Mind,"* which can only be in perfection, because the Master is the Only perfect. Every thought you think or, breath you take or, every happy or angry feeling you have is seen, heard, and felt, by the *"All Seeing, All Hearing, Forever Patient Master. He Resides in You, It is You!"* He has been there all along. Life's pains will make you strong. The Master told me, *"Step right up and be a man, cause you'll need faith to understand, cause I was just saying for you to hear, Keep Your Head In Faith Atmosphere."* He resides in me, and you. Feel him, love him, learn him and respect and honor him. Each time we dishonor or disrespect another, we do the same to *"The Master."* There is no escaping this clear truth. It does not matter what religion you call yourself, I am not talking about religion, or something man made. I am talking about what *God, The Creator, Infinite Intelligence, The Supreme Being, Jehovah, Allah, "The Master"* made. I am speaking of THE GREAT ALL, isness, being, and that which you are!

As long as you struggle with language and what name others call the *Mighty Creator* by, you will not have true peace; you will violate your own trust that you made with the *All Powerful.* You can have no peace because you have a *"Judgmental Spirit"* if you insist on devaluing others because you refuse to understand a name or point of view foreign to your own. A judgmental spirit is the result of *Low Self-Esteem.* When you have true value in your life, you realize that you are life, and that same greatness of life is everyone's, no matter where they live or what race, creed, religion or title they claim. When you come into your peace, you will also come into *"Flow"* with all things. You don't judge and wish others to see it your way; you become a part of *"The Great Way of The Master."* You are powerful beyond anything that you can think of or imagine; all you have to do is BE and it will be done! This is what I call, *"Peace In Flow."* You are at peace and have so much of it in your life that, "you flow like water in a live stream, which is full of life." You become conscious of peace and you embed peace into your subconscious mind, by conscious effort and personal will. You attract people of the same type of mind to your reality, because we can only attract that which we are. Peace is the goal and your peace will show in your character, your style and you will be a person of poise and excellent posture.

The Little "Running" Child In My Soul

There was a little child that was about three feet tall that used to run from my laundry closet to my bedroom whenever anyone was over or when I was home by myself. My niece came to visit one day and she asked, "*Who was that?*" I asked, "*Who was what?"* She said, "A little child just ran from the laundry closet to through the hall." I did not know how to explain it; I thought that it was my two or one year old son, the problem was this, "They were asleep!" It happened three years before anyone of them were born also! It happened again after they were born, because that is when my niece asked the question. The little child would always appear out of the corner of the eye. I knew that this little child was harmless. For some reason I did not fear the child at all. I would talk to the child and say, it's alright, and peace is on you. Then I was suddenly afraid and I yelled at the child and said, "If you are not going to be open, then get out of my house!" "I command you in God's name to get out of my house!" If you are not going to reveal yourself like a good visitor, you are not welcomed!" I have never noticed the child since. My spoken word had driven the friendly little visitor away, "I thought!" The little child was asking me to free him from his fears and sufferings. That little boy was *me,* stepping outside of me, confronting me to do what he had chosen me, (*Tamir)* to do nearly 23 years ago. The drive for freedom and peace from the horrible imprisonment by the *Wolf* and the disease of the mind *(Lycanthropy)* which created it, was so strong that my soul stepped up to show me myself, that I may free myself. I am well aware of the fact that some of my readers will stop at this point and think that this is very different; I am sure it is, but let me challenge you to look at your self deeply and be totally honest with your self and you will discover some things that will make you see how powerful that thing call *soul and spirit* is; there are many times that things occurred that you cannot seem to explain, yet you felt that you were an intimate part of whatever went on. You were! It seems that the first inclination of human beings is to deny what they do not understand or refuse to accept. However, that is the same trait of those whom we label as failures. Isn't that ironic? Isn't it ironic that people who always have to have *"proof,"* or see results before they do or believe something, are part of the 95% to 97% of the people in America and possibly around the world who are dead or dead broke before the age 65?

Have you ever been so deep in thought or in fantasy that you forgot that you were in your living room instead of in the Bahamas? You could smell the water, the air and even taste the food and hear the music. You imagined what you were wearing and you even imagine an endless wallet, or purse, with money to spend on anything you liked. At that moment, you were actually *(a mental picture of you, created by you)* there! As long as you gave conscious to those thoughts, you were in that reality or, you created another entity and a probable reality. Now, imagine some of the things that you have done either subconsciously and unconsciously and then have come to realize it later. Now ask yourself, *"Is my little child running, crying, hurting, laughing, scared and trying to get my attention?"* Would you allow your biological child to go hungry or suffer pain that was in your power to stop or alleviate? Of course not; it is your duty to do the same with the little one inside, but even more so. Your very survival or sanity depends on it. Your little child is who you are. Your little child is your blissful, wondrous, most imaginative, fantasy, incredible self. *"Let the Little Child Play."*

Whenever my family and I would visit my in-law's house, I would feel uncomfortable. The bed was hard and I have never gotten a good nights rest there in 16 years. I have spent the night there on many occasions, but never felt rested. I noticed at night when we watched television how the blinds were open, where people could see in if they desired, and the window by the dining area had a curtain that could not be drawn, it gave a very open look, just like my mother in-law wanted it. The window in the kitchen had that same kind of curtain. I would walk up to the house and was always able to look in. *"They were loose and did not understand that people could see you at night and come and rob you."* Theses were my thoughts and they were dominating my mind. Before I went to bed in their house, I would lock all the doors and close the blinds that were able to be closed. I would not go into the back room to sleep, until I was just too tired to stay awake. I always felt vulnerable with unlocked doors and open blinds or curtains. The *Wolf Man* would surely see me. This was all subconscious; I was actually *"The Wolf Man,* my own worst enemy*!"* My siblings had created a monster and I blamed my parents for not protecting me from the horrors and sufferings that I endured. They were not there to protect me. I forgive them, because they had their own *Whisperer* to deal with; they would never knowingly do harm to any of their children.

The Dawn Visitor

One night, the day after thanksgivings 2004, I was at home alone. I left the hall light on and locked all the doors, closed every blind and locked every window in the house. When I showered, whether someone was home or not, I would lock the bathroom door, and I would not close my eyes in the shower because, I knew that one day, someone would appear. I went to bed after my shower and made sure that the bathroom door in my bedroom was closed, my closet door had to be closed, because my attic entrance is in the master bedroom, and someone could come out of the attic or be hiding up their. Somehow I manage to sleep but would always wake up in the middle of the night, sometimes drenched in sweat. Sometimes I would wake up and yell. I would turn the house alarm chime on, so if and when someone came in, the alarm would say, "Door open." The alarm gave me a sense of security, because, after all, people need alarms these days, right? But, one night I was dreaming that I had got up to wake up the house as my wife would call it. She used to open up all the curtains and windows and let the light of life come in. I would say, "It is too early; let us have some privacy first." But getting back to my dream, I went to open the kitchen curtain, and then I proceeded to open the sliding door blinds and something said, "turn around!" when I turned, I saw a man! He peaked around the corner about 15 feet away from me and within a flash he was in my face. He was a slender or thin white man between fifty and sixty years old, about five feet seven inches tall, and with some gray hair. He did not say a word. I yelled and hit him and said, "Get the Bleep out of here!" I woke up. The next night I was still horrified, and slept with all the lights on. Whenever I went to my office to study, before and after this event, I would close the door. For the 3 months following my dream, I would look in the direction from which the stranger had come, all the while thinking that he would reappear, and *"he most certainly did!"* When I prayed, I would close the office door, and I would always sit with my back against a wall. In my mind lingered the thought that someone could see me or come from behind me to do something to me, right? I am from Chicago and we had to survive! These were survival skills. In addition, it is incumbent on a man to protect his family. But who was this man, this stranger in my dreams? Why was this man in this dream so different from all of my other dreams? What did this all mean and why did he peak around that corner like that? The Wolf man in the old movie peaked around a tree in the fog before he attacked a victim; had I just been victimized? Strangely, I did not feel like this visitor was someone who would hurt me. I was afraid, and I wondered why he had come to me in my dream. The pieces were not all together yet and they would not be until a full 2 months later on February 26th 2005.

After many years of toil and struggle, and 12 months of more intense reading, and the national company convention I would recite, "I attract affirmations," given to me by my friend. He *(The Master)* said, write, *"I Attract people that are willing, able and ready to do my business."* I then took it to this level and would read these two and sometimes three times per day with emotion and feeling,

"What the mind can conceive, and believe the mind can achieve!"

How Do I Acquire That State of Mind That Attracts Riches and Peace Of Mind?

I Am Certain That,
I have acquired that state of mind, which attracts peace of mind. I have that state of mind now, today!

I have high self-esteem and self-confidence; I "will" and I do attract people with high self esteem, and self-confidence, and a great sense of awareness to my life Now, today!

I am Certain that,
I will and I do attract harmonious people, circumstances and things that are willing to work with me, in my life, to my reality now, today!

I have a "personal magnetism," that draws and attracts people to me now, today, people that desire to work with me now, today at this very moment!

I Am Certain That,
I "will" and I do attract People who will persist, until they succeed to my reality, in my life now, today, with little or no effort from me.

I will not be denied
I am peace, I am sweet, and I am serene now, today, with little or no effort from me.

I Am Certain That,
I "will" and I do attract people and things that are good Now, today! I attract only the good to my family, those I love and to my house, now, today! The Creator (The Master) is always with us and only good can reside in our heart and soul and our physical dwellings.

I Am Certain
That, I "will" and "do" have a Great and wonderful attitude everyday of the year. I am peace, I am sweet, and I am serene, with little or no effort from me.

I Am Certain now, today that,
Anything that is not consistent with goodness from The Creator of All Things, God, The One True Master, can never come near me or those I love no matter where we are. I am peace, I am sweet and I am serene.

Peace Be Upon You

I will not be denied peace, sweetness, gentleness and serenity. I am that calmness of mind.

What Can I Do To Become, "Sweet, Peaceful and Serene Now, today, with little or no effort from me?

I am peace, I am sweet, and I am serene.

"I Have Perfect Harmony In My Life Now, Today!"

"I will allow to enter my mind, no person's opinion, no influence which does not harmonize with my purpose."

NOW, TODAY, "I, CLOSE THE DOORS TO MY PAST," I shut out any regrets, frustrations or bitterness or post-mortems.

I FORGIVE MYSELF AND OTHERS FOR ANY AND ALL PAST EXPERIENCES, OFFENSES AND TRANSGRESSIONS. I LEARN A LESSON FROM PAST MISDEEDS

"Every adversity has within it the seed of an equivalent or greater benefit."

For 12 months I read like I had never read before. I sought, looked, enquired, searched and would not be denied. I heard Jeffery Combs in the Spring of 2004, and I was attracted to his style. He reminded me of my mother saying, *"Thoughts are things and your words are powerful."* 6 months after my first introduction to Jeffery Combs, I decided to listen to him again. I listened exclusively to the 4 tape series called, *"Mindset Consciousness."* I replayed the series for approximately 10 times in a 2 week period. I was intrigued by the power of the language as I always have been. There was something about Jeffery Combs that impressed me. Then one day, while one of my business partners was in Barnes and Nobles book store, he met Jeffery Combs! Talk about things happening for a reason. My business partner said, Tamir, "I met this guy named Jeffery Combs." In response, I said, "Man, I have been listening to that guy for 2 weeks straight." This incident prompted me to search for and call the number on the back of the taped package. I discovered that the phone number was a local number, and that Jeffery Combs lived fewer than 5 miles away from me. Until that moment, I had never noticed his address on the tape packet. He returned my call, and I was truly awe struck. He attended our convention for which he had been booked sometime before. This was getting good and I knew that something special was about to happen, but I did not have a clue as to what. Everything I did with Jeffery Combs from that point on was to impress him; to show that I was somebody, who really felt like nobody because of the terrible blows to my *self-esteem.* I was not aware of it at all. *Gary* was aware, but *Tamir* had not delivered the defining blow to *"The Whisperer."* I had been hearing this song in my head for years, *"look what happened to Gary." It would always be melodious and heart felt. Then I would hear my mother's voice, "Gary, Gary time to come home."* I have heard these vibrations for years. *Gary* was reminding *Tamir* that *"we must breakthrough now."*

I Found Peace within Me

I stepped outside of my door one clear, beautiful morning in late winter and something was different; I thought, "This feels good." Like a child, it's beautiful again! The Blossoms were beautiful, the taller trees were beautiful, and the clouds, the sky the ground and the air were different. I did not understand it, but it seemed like I had stepped into another dimension. I most certainly had! I looked outside it was February 13th 2005; I could see little particles swimming like fish in the sky. Everywhere I turned; there they were, floating, moving, diving and full of energy. I had never noticed this before. These little swimming particles seemed to be happy and just full of energy and vigor; they were definitely alive and they danced across the sky, and into my eye. I felt like I was in touch with the universal order of things and that I was growing to another level of being. It was and is beautiful! Beauty seemed to radiate from everywhere, and from everything; the air was beautiful, and my thoughts were joyous and pure. *Keep Your Head to the Sky, for the clouds to tell you why, "They surely will tell you why.* The winds and the rains were beautiful; my soul stood up and delighted in my awareness of my *being ness, is ness, my I Am Ness.* I felt free and without burden or strain for the first time. I touched that realm of beauty that I had not touched since I was about 5 years old or younger. I felt peace for the first time in nearly 40 years. What did all this mean? What was happening with me, in my being? What strange force had I tapped into? What force or power had I summoned from deep within that suddenly dawned on me? Still, the pieces were not together and none of it made sense, in fact I did not know that any sense was to be made of it. I thought it interesting but the time was not right. The ego still had its seat as the king and high priest in my life.

Two weeks later February 24th, 2005 I went to a seminar called, "*Breakthroughs to Success.*" Jeffery Combs was the seminar leader. The first night we had an awesome reception at Jeffery Combs' home. I went around the house mingling with everyone that I could, while seeking to establish my dominance as the man, the myth and the legend in all of my low self-esteem glory; I was broke also! Here I am at the most important event of my life, the defining moment of my life, after nearly 40 years of hell, and I perform up to task and licked my chops. I sized up everyone and said, "I can do this." On the second day, during one of the sessions, I said something that I had no idea that I would say. I said, "*I came to find out why I am an under-achiever.*" I do not know why I said that, because that had never crossed my mind in all of my life. That same evening during an exchange, I made a statement which prompted Jeffery Combs to seize the moment, and ask, "Are you married, do you have commitment issues?" I exploded and said, "My family does not have anything to do with this, and I would thank you to leave them out of it!" I made the statement with so much rage and anger that my secret was out. Everyone had seen the *Wolf Man* in me! Jeffery immediately turned away from the beast. He knew some of what was inside of me, but he had to expose me to everyone else so that the victory could be won; I had to be willing to free myself. My pain became obvious to me and apparent to others. I said, I apologized for breaking the rule not to hurt anyone during the session, and blamed my outburst on my anger and frustration." Jeffery Combs had already shown *the beast and the deliverer.* The lid was masterfully removed and the beast had no shelter. The only shelter he actually had, was the ego's hard shell, otherwise, neither the beast nor any unwanted character could hang around for long. It must have your permission. I not only gave the beast permission, I gave it the keys, the deed, the family and everything else that meant anything to me.

My soul had been shaken. I did not know or understand how I could allow myself to be taken like that in front of all those people. To hide my embarrassment, I sought validation, made excuses, and bragged about how I made him (Jeffery) back up, which he had done. I went home that night feeling uneasy, because I knew that my façade, my mask was no longer there. Everyone had seen me for who I was or for who I was pretending to be. My *self-esteem* was shot and had suffered a crushing blow in front of the world; and I sought answers in my prayers. I woke up around 5:30 a.m. the following morning and I prayed and read a chapter called *"Serenity,"* from As A Man Thinketh, by James Allen. I had read this book and this chapter about 50 times over the past 90 days. It said, *"Calmness is power; self-control is mastery, say unto your heart, "Peace Be Still."* I became calm, serene and sweet. Little did

I know that the event of the night before, had paved the way for rebirth.

I went to the seminar for the third day and instantly people noticed and commented on my calm and peace. It was like magic. I did not know why and/or for what I was prepared. My first thoughts were to not to return to the seminar after my *self-esteem* had been hit, by the revelation of the beast, *The Wolf Man* within me. The *Whisperer* made a last effort to get me not to come back and justify it. It did not work; my peace was my calm and *The Master Awakened!* Later that day, I volunteered to speak openly about me in a group setting; about 15 seconds into the reason for my being there, someone said, *"That's bull sh--"* You are always trying to impress people with your big words and the fact that you write books. We can all see through you!" One lady said, "I wish you would shut up. You have such an ego." People seemed to take delight in telling *the beast* how uncomfortable he made them feel. Jeffery Combs said, *"Do you know what your problem is? You have high self-confidence and low self-esteem. You are a handsome young man. You dress well and you are very creative, everyone knows how creative you are; why do you try to impress me? You sent me a book with no cover on it. 'Without allowing me to respond, he continued,' Man, I respect you already, you don't have to impress me." Someone else said, "We all see how phony you are, it's all about you and we can all see you."* The *Wolf Man* as trapped. I did not fight, and I did not run for the first time in my adult life. I was in a circle and I was caged like an animal, just like the animal that was inside of me, *"The Wolf Man."* I was asked to address those comments and I said, *"I am valuable, and because of this, I do not need anyone's approval. I am just what you see in me now, this very moment, and I do not need to be, or want to be anything else, but the natural me." I went on to say, "Now if you do not like me, that's fine. I am just plain Tamir with no fluff or show to put on and I love myself."* At that point Jeffery asked, *"Is this what you came for?"* I said, "Yes." Jeffery said, *"Everybody give him a hug."* I have never felt the same since. For the next few days, I confronted that *Whisperer,* and now the exposure is full. When my wife picked me up at the end of the seminar, she looked at me and commented a day later, *"You look like you have been crucified."* For the next two and a half weeks I cried while I typed away at my computer. My mind took me all the way back and showed me my life and how things came to be the way they were. Things were never the same from that point on in my life.

The *"Dawn Visitor,"* was none other than *Jeffery Combs*. He came to tell me that my deliverance was at hand. I did not know this then but, if you think back at the description of the visitor in my dream, it will all make sense. I do not only believe what I just wrote, but I *know* it, and have never been more certain about anything else in my life." Why didn't I know or recognize the visitor in my dream before this event? My answer is this, *"the student was not quite ready."*

The Master Told Me One Day, That I'd Find Peace In Every Way

I have that peace, and now I am a success in my being. If you knew how it felt to be successful, "dear reader," you would be in a hurry to get there, to get the peace and happiness that I feel right now. If you knew what I now know, you would read the books, attend those seminars, and listen to the tapes and audio programs available to you. You would do these things over and over again for however long it takes. There is no man on earth that can give me anything in exchange for this feeling. *Those who know are already successful! Gary* created his own champion for peace that would stand up to the *Whisperer* who created the *Wolf Man,* and he withdrew after he had accomplished the deed. *Gary* was strong and powerful, a young child with the heart of a lion, and the vision of an eagle. All the creativity came from *Gary.* It was he, who orchestrated the whole thing for his own deliverance from the fruits of evil, as word which if turned around says, *"live." The Master Had Awakened!* Now, Whisperer, "there is hell to pay!" I have dedicated my life to exposing your coward, manipulative murderous intent. You intended to steal from mankind the peace love and happiness that are his by divine inheritance. I walked in the light after my breakthrough, I began to really take notice of the sun and its glorious splendor; the flowers seemed to speak to me and the winds carried me to other thought worlds. There is a joy that I feel that cannot be described in words; you must experience yours for yourself. However, I can provide some assurance that such enlightenment exist for everyone.

Tamir Qadree "With Gary"

In taking on the name, *"Tamir Qadree," Gary* was left out. He orchestrated the victory over his 40 year imprisonment; his name deserves to be mentioned and to be mentioned first. He was the first and he appeared last! *Gary* heard the call, *"The Creator is The Greatest,"* and was decisive when he first heard, *"Keep Your Head to the Sky,"* and he knew what he desired and never abandoned it. That is why the name of the author on the cover is *Tamir Qadree, "With Gary."*

What's In a Name?

The names chosen are descriptive of what was to take place for freedom from self-imprisonment. The names denoted the actions that I was to take to get and have peace and happiness. The power of the name, of words, is a tremendous force and must not be taken lightly. I believe that the subconscious or the soul knows what it needs However, you must direct it, before the subconscious will do your bidding. The number one question now becomes, *"what's in a name?"* In a name there is life, liberty and whatever characteristics you desire. For centuries, eastern cultures, islanders and others have given their offspring names that spoke to their soul;

characteristics and attributes that they felt would define the life of the infant. Names like, *"Rising Sun, Great Eagle, The Patient, The Prosperous and Fruitful, The Loving, The Gentle, Long Lived* and so on. Take a look at the culture and customs around the world and you will notice this amazing pattern of naming children with action directing names. In western society, names are typically given just because of sound or passed on because of family tradition, but, no thought is given to the meaning and the personality that the name has the power to instill in the child. With this understanding, names are chosen in some communities around the country to direct the subconscious in a better, more excellent direction. However, no matter how excellent a name is, if you do not develop the characteristics of the name from the *inside,* you may as well not have it. In fact, your name is actually determined by the way you think, act and respond to circumstances and/or experiences. I ask people, *"what is your name?"* I then listen, watch and observe, so that I can discover what their *real or true* names are. I will not be convinced, in spite of how many times you try to tell me that a car or a truck is a duck. Until that car or truck quacks, wobbles or grows a beak like a duck, it will always be a car or truck to me. What is your name? What does your name mean? Now ask your self, "How do I behave and what am I thinking about daily?" Then you will discover your real or true name. Now you can begin living, and I mean, "Truly living." I challenge every one of you to ask yourself those questions, and I will guarantee that, if you are sincere with yourself and forthright, you will feel and see the world differently. Your thoughts will change, which in turn will trigger your actions to change and then, presto; *"Your outer circumstances must change."* This is so basic, yet so far from the average person's mind, that I am more intrigued by it even as I write this. Something as seemly simple as a name, is ignored for entire lifetimes, yet names can be the most powerful tool for your growth and peace of mind. Names are free and clear to anyone that desire to have one, or change one, or even add one. The best part about it is this, *"It is all up to you and you can call the shot anyway you desire!"* I am not suggesting that you change your name, and I am not hoping that you do. The goal is to *"awaken"* in you something greater than you can imagine at this time in your life and career. Knowing that you are a powerful, dynamic and creative being, and living up to that fact is the stuff that miracles are made of. What we are, and what we become, are forged by what we speak, the dreams and desires we have, are a symphony of what's inside. They play our lives out, miserable or blissful, they play indeed!"

May The Master Awaken Within You All, and May You Find That Special Place That Dwells Beneath The Tempest, Beyond The Reach Of Mental and Spiritual Turmoil; In The Eternal Calm Now, This Day And In This Time.

Chapter 4 The Walk Through Life

It was through no fault of my own that I suffered from this terrible disease, *(Lycanthropy)* but, to be free, it was my duty to liberate my self with the help of those who were put in my path for that purpose. All the pieces fell into place, and into perfect sequence. I did what I knew how to do, while at the same time I had no clue as to what I was searching for; I sought peace, stillness and happiness.

I heard a wise woman say, "*The way you strut and your gait are often through no fault of your own.*" We are creatures of habit and influence. The earth is soft and impressionable, and so are the minds of human beings. When you can see the light in the dark and see the stars in the light, you will have witnessed another reality, a surer reality! The stars represent your shining through the darkness. The stars give you hope and assurance that you are on course to the desires of your heart. You are truly a shining star, no matter who you are! My experience is an example of this; let it propel you to your deepest aspirations. If you feel that you have no dreams I will say, "That is simply not accurate!" Your dreams and aspirations have just been lost, stolen or thoroughly hidden from you, but you do have the seeds of greatness in you. Say to your self, "I have greatness in me!" Say it with feeling and really believe it. Write it down, read it 10 times per day for 90 days and watch what will happen. You will start to discover things that you love, that you have not thought of or mentioned in years, and you will start to see things around you differently. You will jump-start your mind, *your servant,* to think for you, and not to just drag you along, like it had been doing for all your years. If you still feel that you do not have life dreams and aspirations, you must now know that you have been in a game, but instead of playing in the game, you have been used as the sheepskin, or the ball. That can never be fun. Imagine being passed around and kicked, slammed through a hoop, slammed out of a baseball park 400 feet to deep center, or slapped with a stick through a fishermen's net, while fans cheer for more of your blood. When you are too worn, the referees will exchange you for some other person with no aspirations and do the same to them. Have you ever seen a sporting event where the officials ran out of balls to play the game? Let me give you a little tip. *"It never happens!"* Why? Because 95% percent of the population will stand up and demand to *"be the ball!"* The other 5% demands to have the ball. That 5% will say, *"Give me the ball!"* The choice is yours and yours alone. Let me caution you; "the longer you are employed with little or no pay, as a "*ball or an object,"* of someone's pleasure, you instill in your subconscious mind that this is the natural way of life. Your subconscious, (*which is power without direction)* will see to it that you have every opportunity to remain employed. *Back, Back, Back, Way Back... "It's a home run; 400 feet to center field!"* Now, some of you may not like the insinuations or my remarks at this point, however, only those who feel guilty will feel this way; that is not all bad, in fact it is not bad at all. Now you have something to work on and say to yourself, "I will tell that Tamir something and I will show him a thing or two." Good, *"it's about time that we get to see and be graced with your greatness."* You are no longer a *holdout; You* can now become an *all-out.*

Chapter 5 Self-Esteem

Self-esteem is something that we all need. We all need to constantly nurture it and appreciate its value to life. Just as the seed sown in the soil requires sunshine and water, so Self-esteem requires faith, commitment and peace of mind to grow and to be healthy. These are the sunshine, water and nutrients to our self-esteem. Money may not be your issue, success may be something that you feel that you already have, or you may have written books on *self-esteem,* that is all fine and dandy. However we all still need *self-esteem* everyday. The more we learn and accept ourselves for who, what and where we are, the more we are given and the more we reinforce our *self-esteem.* Just as the sun rises daily, as surely as we need daily bread and water, "we need daily boosts to our *self-esteem*!" We can get it through prayer, meditation, singing, reading, poetry, painting and a multitude of ways, but, one thing is for sure, *"we all need it!" Self-esteem* is the great equalizer. The next time you witness someone flashing or showing off their worldly possessions or boasting about their accomplishments, you can rest assured that you have just witnessed low or a bruised *self-esteem* in action. The next time you meet someone who has to boss others around and always be right and just cannot go a day without controlling someone else's affairs, you have just witnessed a person who has *self-esteem* issues. The next time you hear someone indulged in sexually explicit and degrading verbiage, you are witnessing low *self-esteem." These are often signs of compensating for other issues and concerns.* I challenge you to challenge yourself and read this book, not once, but twice; recommend it to as many people as you can speak too! If you can purchase more than a few copies, do so, because this is a gift that will go on long after you are dust and bones and forgotten about or not. When you read the first chapter or the one following, you will not be the same! Even if you decided to put it down and never finish the reading, the portion that you do read or have read, will be in your subconscious mind and you must take some action or your *self-esteem* will let you know. *The Creator of All Things,* made you with *value and manifestation.* He created you with all the tools to manifest the glory of *"God"* within you. It is the biggest tragedy of life to ignore your greatness and not to explore the possibilities dormant within you. Let your creative imagination and genius flow like the great rivers of the earth. If you do, some of us will enjoy just sitting on the banks and watching the wondrous flow of the life that you manifest. You might ask, "What gives you the boldness to write such a book, covering the different aspects of life and self-esteem?" I have over 40 years of memorable experience to back up my writings. I have lived what I write and I write what I live; I come from the core of my being and when that is done, no outside approval is warranted.

On February 26th 2005, my soul danced, my soul stood up straight, and the sun shone clearly on me that day. My burdens are light, my dark nights are guides and my adversities are my messengers of hope, faith, peace of mind, happiness and the great things that are to manifest in my life. When I speak of self-esteem, I am speaking of myself, but more importantly to you, "*I am speaking of you!*" It does not matter who you are or what status you hold in life; it does not matter if you have high self-esteem or if you are an NBA basketball superstar with millions of dollars. In all actuality we all desire to feel valuable. The simplest thing to remember is this, *"Nothing Really Matters,"* in the final or grand scheme of things; nothing really matters outside of us, because the outside is only a reflection of what is really inside. So the next time you find yourself feeling poor in spirit and feeling that you are not as worthy as the next person, remember that life is a journey of discovering *"who you really are,"* and in that you will find your true value, which is immense. Everything else does not really matter. Please do not take the last sentence lightly. Read it and re-read it again and again, until you can go into it and under it, to really feel what it means. Too much time is spent on things that make little difference, and too little time is spent on things that matter the most. What is there that can be more valuable than peace of mind, love, abundance and happiness in your soul? What can you tell yourself in your mirror that will be of greater importance than these? What can be more profound, than going into the quiet abode of your own mind and, connecting with that all powerful source that many call God, The Creator, The Supreme being, Allah, the Great ALL and many other names? By understanding the above sentence, thinking, acting and living with this in mind, you will have a healthy self-esteem. You will change the rate of your vibrations, you will feel lighter, and you will attract the best things in life, provided that you desire them.

Self-Esteem "Busters"

"Use tact, be diplomatic, be nice, keep it positive and find a better way to say it." "You don't want to offend anyone; Keep the door open for future relationships or transactions." Never burn your bridges, and you shouldn't do this or that, or you have to be this or that."

All of the above have been said over and over again to me for most of my life. After hearing those things so many times, believe me, "I did not know how to respond naturally to anything. My life was a bunch of "don't say this that way," and "You should have done this or said that." What I did was decide that I must conform to what I was hearing, since, after all, it was dealing with people properly and professionally with tact that bred success, right? Well, I bought that stuff and before I knew it, I was not me and did not know how to be, or discover the real me. You see, all of my teenage and adult life, people have been diplomatic with me and smooth with me and pleasant to me, until they forgot that the aim was to assist me. The best way to assist me would have been for each person to be himself or herself, maybe then I could locate my self and be a better person. The pattern of destruction starts when we speak from the head and not from the heart. In the head you might come up with some beautiful sounding words and phrases that have little real influence on who you are addressing. Coming from the heart is *"Keeping it real."* I am more into *"Keeping It Real,"* than I am about tiptoeing around, and trying not to offend anyone or saying the wrong words. That is called Fear; fear of loosing someone, some thing, or some reputation that you have built. I had trouble keeping it real, because it had been instilled in me that I was not diplomatic and that I had to become this or that. In other words, *"who I was, was never good enough and I had to change it."* Naturally, I worked my *"rear-end"* off to fit into society's mold, (which really did not fit me,) but it did do major damage to my already ailing self-esteem. I have since learned that, "*I can be me!"* When you come from your peace and inner harmony, you can be you and speak what comes from your heart, without stopping to think about your words. When you speak from the heart, you speak from the core of your being. If your core is peace and happiness, it will come forth. I have had people say to me, *"You are a good man; you are speaking to me out of love and consideration."* The person that said this to me was just told how much fear I saw in him and how low his self-esteem was. I had just given him a cold slap in the face and instead of him being offended; he appreciated my love and consideration. I did not coat anything, I said what I felt and he felt my heart and my peace. What if I had done the old, *"be diplomatic thing,"* and ignored being me? I would have been doing the gentlemen a great disservice. Instead, by coming and *"Keeping It Real,"* my remarks may have life changing effects on his life; my remarks were medicine to his subconscious mind, because they gave him something to consider deeply. That is what happened to me, as you will continue to discover in this book. Someone kept it real and told me like it was, and not how I wanted to hear it. This is not the only such incident that I can relate, but it is a fine example of the point that I am making here. Let's be clear and to the point. I am all about *love, peace, happiness, self-control, and being a dynamic and pleasing personality.* However, I can only accomplish this personality by being comfortable with who I am. Whatever you decide to be, *"Be You and Be Real."* Opportunity seeks out those who are real and genuine; opportunity avoids those who are fake and plastic.

The Shouldn't

"You shouldn't say this or shouldn't do this, or you S*hould* have done this or that." Will someone tell me what this "*Should-have"* stuff is all about? Where did it come from and where is it going? I am tired of people *Shouldn't* on me! I don't even *"Should*" on myself; I am certainly not going to allow anyone else to give me there bag full of *Shouldn'ts. Should*, takes you out of what you do, and out of your free expression. How can you freely express yourself and your talents and feeling, with this *"Shouldn't"* look over your shoulder and hanging around your neck? It's a wonder how anyone can get anything done when this "*Should"* gang shows up. Here is a secret, a big secret; "The *Should* people are generally the biggest procrastinators." "*Should,"* always sets up procrastination, and procrastinators are indecisive. Indecisiveness is an enemy to achievement. The next time someone says, "I am thinking about what I *"Should"* do, or if I *"Should"* do this or not," take a mental step to the side and duck for cover, because procrastination usually comes afterwards. Now, all this advice about the word "should" is good information and I am sure that it will serve you well. Now, I would like to give you a few words and phrases that can replace "*should.*" Instead of saying "I Should have..." say, *"How can I improve on my actions or performance?"* Instead of saying, "I shouldn't have..." said, *"What can I do to make this a different situation, or have a more desirable outcome?"* Instead of saying, "I *Should* Talk to so and so," ask yourself, *"Who can I talk to concerning or about this issue?"* Instead of saying, "we *Should,"* say, *"how or what do you feel about going here and doing this or that."* I realize that this can take some time getting used to, but it is well worth the discipline involved, in getting your mind to shift your paradigm, and strengthen your self-esteem. You will feel better about yourself, after you have released the burden of *"Should,"* which carries the burden of *guilt and shame.*

False-Esteem

False-Esteem is a term that I coined, because of experiences that I have had more than once in my life. There are times in my life when I would subjugate my true value to fit into someone else's scheme, while neglecting my own powerful self worth. The reason for this was simply that, I wanted, and craved recognition. I did things that catered to other peoples' whims, plans and fancies for attention and praise. These actions gave me a *"False"* feeling of value and importance. Worst still, it created in me a desire to always look outside of me for validation. That validation gave me a false sense of importance and self-worth. That is what I call, *"False-Esteem."* The validation gave me so much false worth, until the real me, like an onion, was wrapped up with layers upon layers of it. It is important that you learn to unwrap the layers around your true self; the following chapters in this book are designed to assist you in doing just that. *Keep reading and you will discover something about yourself, that only you can discover for yourself.*

Hype-Esteem

Hype-Esteem is when what you do or think is overly praised, or when you are given credit for some things that are not totally the way it is told or said. I was a "*Hype-Attic,"* in that I would perform at jobs, networking events and on other occasions, just for the hype of it all. My *self-esteem* was so damaged that, I needed this *"Hype-Esteem"* to help me to feel good, or important; or like I was making a huge contribution to whatever I was working with. Whenever the time came, that I was not part of the main show, or my name was not mentioned, I would feel down. I felt like I had to perform up to someone else's standards to get the *"Hype"* or be recognized as someone important. All the while, I was feeding an addiction called, *"Hype-Esteem."* Whenever some event, or happening outside of you is the reason that you feel, act, and think important, "your *self-esteem* is seriously injured." I have experienced this roller coaster of *"Hype- Esteem*" for many years. In every sales position, or non-sales position that I have ever had. I would be up and up with "*Hype-Esteem,"* and totally down, down when the praise or recognition was not there. The truly remarkable thing is that, the Hype was always provided by someone other than me. Someone else always pulled the strings, preying on my competitive spirit and drive, and on that of others. I had very little self-control. I learned to feel good about myself without the Hype, and you will learn to do the same for yourself. It is all about "*Freeing The Self." Hype and False-Esteem can never cause you to be free!* When you are free, you can flow in motion.

For more on healthy esteem visit
www.esteemnow.com

Chapter 6 Self-Improvement

To be self-improved is to be self-approved. When you understand the latent value with which you were born, you will operate, vibrate and live from a different perspective. When you were born, The *Creator* gave or infused you with all the value you will ever require. Every book, painting, song, dance, laugh and whatever you are to do, and to be, has always been with you. You can command whatever you desire and receive it, you must demand whatever you desire, because it is inherently yours. Society says, "Get a job, fit into this or that scheme and you will be successful." Be an athlete, or a movie star or an inventor, and then you will be approved. Are these things really what you have a deep desire in your soul to be, do or have? Or, are the things that someone else planned for your life, for their life fulfillment and purpose?

"Once you figure out if a desire is yours for you, and not to fit into someone else's plan for you, you will automatically feel a certain peace of mind come over you and through you."

Self-Improvement is self-realization, and self-acceptance, which needs no outside approval. When you are flowing with the power within you, all the answers to life are with you. Your studies, books, seminars and tape programs, are all guides that assist you on the way to self-discovery, discovery of the real you. We learn through Self-Suggestions that may be influenced by external forces, and also through Autosuggestion. This is a reality, we cannot escape, nor should we want to. Every thing that you experience in life serves as a lesson and tool for your growth and self-realization. In realizing who you really are, with out the mask and the facades, you step into your power, your natural powerful selves. You will cease to fuss and fume and allow outside circumstances to dictate your actions and reactions. You will have discovered the True Master *within you*; he has always been there, waiting for your every command. In the Disney production "*Aladdin,*" *Aladdin* would rub the magic lamp and the genie would appear and say, "*Your wish is my command!*" The genie would grant any wish. Your subconscious mind is the same way, *"it will do exactly as you instruct it to do."* You sub-conscious mind does not recognize jokes or mere words without meaning; it will take you seriously and perform to your exact specifications. Aladdin means, *"Upon the cause and effect,"* When you are self-improved you command the genie or the subconscious to awaken and bring this or that into reality. Like a faithful servant, *"your wish is its command."* The wishes are your spoken and unspoken words; they are your thoughts, desires, urges and inklings. We do this willingly or unwillingly! It is Cause and Effect, which never fails and you get what you command. If you don't operate from the suggestions that you desire and that you give your mind, someone else will direct your mind and you will be a slave to that outside influence. I know of several people who always complain about pains in the body and everywhere they can think of. It is draining to listen to this type of stuff, especially when you are of the understanding that these pains and illnesses are a product of our minds. They were created from impure and wretched thoughts, angry, violent and thoughts of resentment, jealousy and all fears; they manifest in our limbs, arteries and our entire nervous system. Wholesome and clean thoughts manifest into peaceful conditions, free of illness and disease. Worries have been known to make people sick. I will use myself as an example of this. I had the filthy habit of biting my nails for nearly 40 years of my life. I had a temper that was monstrous and even frightened me at times. I was known in some circles to bite when I quarreled, but my language was worst. I would use invectives that should have been not only immoral, but also illegal. I was downright nasty with violent words. In the end I would feel remorse, guilt, and shame. My *self-esteem* would take a terrible pounding for weeks thinking about my *"wolf-man"* like temper. Behind it all was a coward. I had allowed my thoughts to degenerate to the level of the beast. I acted out of fear. I was really afraid and my vitriol and biting, when I had physical encounters, were ways of saying, "Stay away." Just like a wild animal in the woods; they are afraid of man and that is why they attack. My thoughts were always fear thoughts, intimidating thoughts, thoughts of lack, loss, limitations and deprivation. That is exactly what I received in my life. My thoughts became manifest in my flesh, and they became *my law or my own making.* I have since changed that. I no longer bite my nails, and for many years, I have had no physical altercations. I do not get angry and out of control, but now display greater self-control. I do not have to do all the talking nor do I have to be right. I do have *"righteous indignation"* when called for, but never out of hate, or anger do I lash out at another individual. I will allow no one to enter my kingdom and get past my vigilant guards and disturb my peace. This is not to say that I am perfect, because I am far from that in the flesh. However, the self-awareness itself and the willingness to be better is elixir to the soul.

The apex of self-improvement, I believe, is peace of mind, happiness, self-control, thought mastery and recognizing that, *"The One True Master"* resides within you. Assume command, and all things are possible for you. When *Jesus* was with his disciples at sea, a great tempest arose and the ship was covered by the waves, but Jesus was asleep. In Matthew 8, verses 24-27, the disciples came to him in a panic. Jesus asked, *"Why are you fearful, oh you of little faith?"* Then he rose and rebuked the winds and the sea; and there was a *Great Calm.* But the men marveled, saying, "*What manner of man is this,* that even the winds and the sea obey him!" The storms and winds of life trials and tests will surely blow; they will cause you to think, ponder and even wonder, however, the strong calm man makes the wind and the storms of life obey him. The eternal calm is where Jesus resided, and so can be with every human being ever born into this reality. That is self-improvement. Jesus gave the example 2000 years ago. Muhammad did it some 1400 years ago, as did Buddha and Confucius before both Christ and Muhammad. Others past and present have been shining examples of the kind of command that makes the winds and storms of life obey them. Today, many people are shinning examples of the power of peace and mastery of thought. What good are material things, if you do not have peace, love and happiness? The material things that you seek, (many of you will claim that you do not seek material) will only increase your burden if you have no peace, love and happiness in your life? The peace, love and happiness brings harmony in your life. Without perfect harmony with the universe and all that the Creator Created, peace of mind is not possible.

The subject of self improvement is not new and is a widely spoken term today. Let's examine one aspect that is grossly overlooked and see how it plays in the game of life, which is a game of improving the self. Physical exercise is important, and so too are thinking, prayer and meditation. One of the overlooked aspects of self improvement is the attention to the body and cleanliness. I am not merely speaking of bathing, showering and basic hygiene; I am going a bit deeper. Perhaps you should receive some insight into that wonderful thing called, "the body." Lets look at it from a different perspective and see what new and exciting ideas will come to your mind as you read and ponder.

Bathing the Body

Many men and women jump into the shower and off they go to work or wherever. Taking baths have become a thing of the past to many people. They are time consuming and showers are just what the fast life of today calls for. Since the body is made, primarily of water, it would make perfect sense to see the importance of merging our bodies with the water of a nice warm bath at least once per week. There is no magic to the number of times you bathe every week. However, the body needs the massaging and soothing, healing effects of the water on the skin and in the pores. The water revitalizes the body and calms the nerves and tissues. The fragrances, (whichever you choose) add pleasant scents made from nature's laboratory. The bones are mellowed and move in a rhythmic way when submerged in water; the mind is calmed and the heart is soothed, while the blood is in perfect flow. When we were in the wombs, we were in water for 9 months. All the value, wisdom, knowledge, growth and maturity that you needed for your life journey was in you, being fashioned and materialized. Taking a bath is more than just physical cleanliness; it is a regeneration of the body, mind and spirit. It is symbolical of the mystical tie of parent and child, of God and Man or the Christ within. It is only in this state can we come back to that state of peace and tranquility that we get away from as we grow into society.

Lotion on the Body

The body is your temple. Treat it well so that it may perform at optimum efficiency. Many men think that it is feminine to put lotion on the body with care and delight. The body requires care and soothing. When you rub your body, you are anointing the body. You are waking up the power in the machine that does your physical bidding. You will put gas in your car, wash it, put oil in it, and rush to get it fixed if it broke down. In contrast, many people will not take the time at least once per week to lotion or oil their entire body. Not a rub here and there, but a careful, 10 minute rub and care for the vehicle that takes care of you. Oh, you will read a book or listen to a tape, attend church service and pray to God for this or that, but many times you will not take care of the great human machine called "The Body." By the way, "your body is a gift and if you neglect it, it will let you know."

The Head

The head deserves to be rubbed and massaged with your fingers. Do not merely rub grease in your hair, find out which is best for you and when you apply whatever hair product on your hair, take the time to massage it in. Dig in with you fingers, it will feel good. You are relaxing the muscles and sending signals to your sub-conscious mind that *"I appreciate you,"* you are also saying, "I care and I will remain loyal to you."

It says to you, *"I am feeling good, and I will carry out your every righteous command."* The head is the crown, your temple. How much respect and honor should you give it?

The Ears and Eyes

The Ears should be massaged and cleaned along the tracts. Your ears should be rubbed and relaxed so that sound may enter without the clutter of every day life. The ears bear witness to your desire and translate them to your subconscious mind, in harmony with your eyes. The Eyes should be rubbed thoroughly in the morning as soon as you wake up. Massaging the vision and circulating the blood makes for clear vision and shows appreciation. Rubbing the eyes and ears communicate to them, *"I am grateful for you and I wish you to do my honest bidding today."* Keep them clean. I recommend more than once per day, and at least upon waking up and again at bedtime. I prefer more than that, but that is my desire. Do as much or as little as you like, but do something. These things are not new, and they are certainly not something that I have made up or have discovered. You have heard these things all of your life; many of you just did not know nor understand what you were hearing or seeing, which leads to actions that are robotic; actions that have lost the greater value.

The Face and Mouth

Along with your eyes, the face is your light. Your mouth is the hollow that speaks the words that create all that you desire in life. A clean, well rubbed, and massaged face will allow your smile to radiate, without struggle. The skin and muscles in the face will speak volumes once cleaned, freshened up and treated like you appreciate it. I have seen beautiful people from afar, but, when I came closer, some were the most undesirable people that I have ever met, and I have seen lovely peaceful, gorgeous people who were shinning with the splendor of the Sun. Washing the mouth and brushing the teeth does more than just give us good smelling breath and shining teeth, it gives us confidence, builds our *self-esteem* and helps us to stand up straight. If you have trouble accepting what I just said, do not brush your teeth or wash you face tomorrow and see how you feel. Go outside to your job or wherever you normally go and see and notice how you feel. If you feel no different, you have some issues that need blasting out. I have designed a special cannon for that sort of issue; I call it the *Super Blaster.*

The Hands, Arms, Legs, Stomach, Chest, Back, Neck and Feet

Every part of our body deserves care and proper treatment. We rarely think in terms of treating the body. We should rub and massage each finger, toe and joint where possible. Where convenient, have someone else, your spouse or mom, assist you in rubbing your back to assure that your entire body is relaxed and appreciated. Remember, you are not merely applying lotion or some ointment to your body; you are treating your entire body. How can you show sincere appreciation for someone else, when you have not learned to appreciate yourself The soul has a rhythm, a *"spiritual guide"* for those who masterfully command with perfect goodness.

Chapter 7 The Whisperer

What got the best of me in my days of temporary defeat was the *self-critic* who always would assault me and then leave, with me holding the bag. It worked every time; like a charm. Until one day, through trial and error, I learned what was going on and I developed, through study and research, ways to combat this *"critical self."* The inner voice we hear that exhort us to some kind of action, be it positive or negative, is at our command. I am convinced that most people do not understand this and many who claim that they do, do nothing about it. Why? They really do not understand. When you understand a thing, you see it from a different perspective, which evokes certain actions which form certain habits to eradicate or strengthens that which you are dealing with. The inner-self will direct you to the appropriate remedy or give you the proper knowledge of how to utilize what you understand. The Whisperer is an enemy to your goals and aspirations. It seeks to undermine your rising. As human beings, our deepest craving is to be appreciated and to feel important. We are all "born" with all the value, excellence, and potential that we need to feel just what we crave deeply. The Whisperer knows this and it tries to undermine your Self-Perception, making you ineffective in the game of life. The Whisperer is a cruel punisher and liar; it is the enemy that sleeps, eats and breathes in you, and you feed it, by allowing it free reign. In a very real sense, the *Whisperer* holds many people prisoner, within their own fortress. The job of the Whisperer is to get you to look at everyone and everything outside of yourself for answers and approval. It will drive you to all kinds of goals, ideals, prophecies and people who will validate your seeking. Others will validate your weakness and admire your guts and drive to be, but, to be what and to do what? To have what? Here is the key, the *Whisperer's* aim is to "*Kill*" you; the natural you, the patent you. Its job is to maim, hurt, put out an eye or two, and weigh down your heart and mind, thereby rendering you ineffectual. It nails the coffin by saying, *"if you don't achieve this or do that in this time frame, like so and so, you are a loser and everyone knows it."* So, the victim moves and acts as if their life depended on the voice of the *Whisperer.* Most victims may even quit and hide, living the rest of their lives suffering and feeling guilty over what they did not accomplish when it was not even their idea or true life desire. The Whisperer laughs and says, *"Another one bites the dust!"* But, there is hope; the Sun shines clear and the Moon will recite what the Sun nurtures and grows.

Read that last sentence again and again.

The Whisperer can only survive and live by "*your*" permission. Quite frankly, you say to it, *"do whatever you will,"* I am not worth anything more than you say I am worth. How would you feel, giving that whisperer a swift kick in the pants? I am speaking of the whisperer that you let in the front door! Yes! The Whisperer that you let in and said, *"Have it your way."* Let's turn the tables and see what will happen. The minute you notice this intruder, (which I am sure that you have already by reading this book) it will take the most drastic, sneaky, sly, repugnant means to hide, run and disguise itself to stay alive and have its way with you. After all, if you have been feeding this Whisperer it has become big and monstrous and will not go away pleasantly. It will kick, scream, yell, cry foul, accuse you of being cruel, call you bad names and everything under the sun to survive. The one thing that is crucial for you to see it this; "it will compliment you and give justification for its use and being with you." *Read that last sentence again.* It will rework, re-word, and re-frame every incident that you discover that it has lied to you about; it will do it under the guise of peace and tranquility.

The first thing that I did when I noticed this intruder was say, "get out of here!" I said it loud and with force, not anger, but righteous indignation. I learned to be firm and to get real with the Whisperer You cannot be nice or soft spoken, you have to be firm and let that trickster know that it is not welcome where you are. When I did this, the thoughts of wrong, deceit and malice or whatever they were, left me at once. Now, I know that it would come back in another form, but the Whisperer knew that it had to change its appearance and revamp. I was ready and was just as desirous of slapping it in the heart again, but this time I would revamp also and do "Bruce Lee" sides kick. Whenever that old ungrateful thing would show up, I would recognize it instantly and quickly guide my thoughts to the direction that I desired. The direction that is most damaging to the Whisperer is *"Peace and Harmony."* The Whisperer can only live and thrive in a chaos evolved environment. When there is chaos and confusion, the Whisperer is strong and dominates the thinking and the life circumstances of the individual. When peace and harmony is the pervading flow in the individual, the Whisperer is weak and cannot afford to stay in that environment. Eventually, it will either submit to peace and harmony, or die of starvation. My goal, for my Whisperer is *"Submission"* to the *Master* that resides within me. There can be no compromise; when a life dwells in the ocean of truth, in the eternal calm. The Whisperer was made out of a vain imagination, therefore it can be made to submit and be peaceful or die of starvation. It can either succeed or fail by being allowed to purify or corrupt the subconscious. That is when *"Mastery of Self-Control"* is attained.

The Whisperer, "In Action or Inaction!"

Let us look at the sales profession or the free enterprise profession. We all know somebody. We are often afraid to, "be somebody," therefore many of us will approach "nobody," and will tell "anybody" how the field of sales or free enterprise did not work for them. The ego says, "I am not valuable!" Therefore, after listening and "agreeing," many people do "nothing," and call it doing "something." After going through this once, and sometimes a few times, many people finally give up and quit altogether, resigning to a life of unfulfilled hopes and dreams. The ego says, "it is not meant for you;" You accept that and say, "I like doing what I do or working my job." That is no more than a lie. Remember the sage advice, *"To*

Thine Own Self Be True?" There is not a human being that ever lived that did not have within the soul the capability and the yearning for enlightenment, a better life, more peace and tranquility. That is the natural order of life. To suggest that you are content with mediocrity is a sham and a farce. The sad reality is that too many people will not face themselves and admit it, let alone work to change it. That is why the title above is *"The Ego in Action or Inaction!"* The action is the ego *"acting"* on your behalf and your acceptance of its damaging advice will cause you to do nothing which is, *"inaction."* The subtle part is that, *"you think that it was your own decision."* This may sound a bit harsh or critical to you but, *"you have been suckered again."* You have gotten so comfortable with that *"lie"* to where you can now waddle in it and claim true happiness, when inside you are crying and decaying. Your soul deserves better and more prosperity and happiness. When will you stand up be a courageous individual and command from your soul, your subconscious, that which you truly desire? You are only afraid either because you believe that you will fail, (Fear of Failure) or you are afraid that you will succeed. *(Fear of Success)* You are thinking, in your mind, "How can I deal with this?" You are saying, "I don't really deserve this, therefore I will create an excuse to avoid it or destroy any possibilities, relationship or whatever has to be done to not allow this to happen." Your self-esteem is shot when this happens, "Shot, but not dead!" You can change it all by first seeing it all and making a decision to change it all and take productive steps in that direction. You can start by reading books on *"Self-Esteem."* You can usually find them at your local library and library cards are free to my knowledge. Another place to start is reading books on "The Ego," in conjunction with the books on Self-Esteem. Do Not Read Them Once! That is like eating once and not eating again for two weeks. **Do Not Be A Mr. or Miss or Mrs. "shy"** when it comes to reading. If reading is difficult for you, start by listening to taped programs on those subjects. You can find great material at the public library and in your local book stores. You can go online to book stores and many other places and ask for what you are looking for and you will find more than you could ever listen to or read. After reading the material, go back and do the assignments in the programs or books. You will find many of them to be more than helpful. If you value your life, *and I know that you do,* you will do whatever it takes to get some good material and start today. *Do Not Stop With This Book.* Let me be the first to say, "I don't have all the answers for you." No one does, so let your search be filled with variety and enjoy the process. When you start, you will discover a love that is true and divine; you will find that having an ego out of control and having low, or very little Self-Esteem simply means, "You have not learned to tap into the great reservoir of LOVE that is within you!" And when you do, as you certainly must, "you will dance a dance that will make the birds sing in greater harmony, because you will hear sounds that you never knew existed. It's All About Love....Yeah! *(With Peace and Happiness)*

Let Flow

(The Whisperer does not like flow)

Things flow "through" you; they do not "come" to you. When you are asking for the thing you desire, you must let if flow; it is not yours to possess. It must remain free, alive, vibrant, life giving, and life enhancing. When you seek to possess or control, the thing you seek, it ceases to be what it is! That is why many do not get what they seek. They get something alright; whenever you instruct your soul, subconscious mind to do something or acquire something, you definitely get something! More often than not, people get something of a different nature, but here is a revelation; "they get what they created!" *Read that line again and ponder it for a few minutes.*

That thing that I have referred to as the "Whisperer" so many times, in the book, is a living thing that thrives off inharmonic maneuvers, chaos, difficulty, stress, struggle, sufferings and *"blunt"* moves with no fluidity, therefore "no flow." The "*Whisperer*" urges you to "*React.*" Reaction does not necessarily mean that the senses are working for your betterment and at the service of others. That is exactly the plan of the *Whisperer*! The plan is to get you to move without any kind of thought, consideration, empathy, love and peace; without listening to your common sense. The key is to learn to "*Respond,*" meaning, *"your senses are working and alert,"* ready to serve you in the most excellent way. The more you are able to *"Respond,"* the more your will create in your being,

"Responsibility." The more responsibility, the more you can *"Re-create."* Now it really gets interesting! What is this *"Re-Create"* thing or stuff?

We shall expound on it here, not in great detail, but in enough detail to cause anyone, learned or unlearned, to think! That is what people need; people need to think more and often. Let us take this word *"Re-create"* and have some fun. The word, "*Recreate,"* comes from the *Latin, "recreates",* pp. of *recreare: To give new life or freshness to: Refresh.* Also, to *form anew in the imagination.* Now, just by taking a look at this definition, you can certainly see the power in this word and the activity that it suggests. Too many would-be achievers do not reach their goal by sheer refusal to relax the mind, take it away and give it drink, food and comfort. How do you do this, you feed it positive things, books, tapes and calming, serene music and melodious sounds. Going to the park with your family and friends and taking in some sports, fishing racing, boating and camping are some forms of "Re-creation." There are many more! There are countless things that one can do to *"form anew in the imagination;"* new things in the mind, which makes a new you. Without refreshing your mind and relaxing your body, you cannot achieve the ultimate goal of *"peace of mind."* When the body goes to sleep, it is natures way of telling you, "We must re-create everyday;" to perform at the optimum. Sleep is the natural *"Re-Creation."* That is not the concern here, instead, the point here is, *"re-creation"* on the conscious level. Your body will go to sleep whether you are willing or not, but choosing to take in *"Re-*

Creation" is solely a matter of choice, thus a matter of keen insight into the workings of the mind. You do not need a *PH. D.* to have this insight; willingness will suffice; and you do not need money to decide.

You see, we "*Re-Create"* everyday; most of us are not aware of what we are actually doing. Everything that the human being needs for surviving, thriving and becoming the beacon of light that we really are intended to be is already *"Created."* What the *"Re-Creation"* does when understood and properly enacted, with conscious effort, is bring about a *"Renaissance," (Rebirth or Revival)* in the soul or life of the human being! We house so much potential that we literally can change our lives in a flash, once we reach that level of being. Do you now understand the value that you have? Do you see that the ego, when commanded properly is not bad? Because its function is to look out for your natural well being. When it is allowed to rule, it rules with tyrannical and deleterious effect on your total life and causes ultimate ruin. That enemy, the "Whisperer" in the mind does not intend rebirth or revival; it only seeks to survive at a cost to you and very dear one. You have to let it submit and be peaceful and in harmony with you; that is the supreme goal that every human being through time will learn if they are to live harmonious, peaceful and happy lives. Please allow me to use, "me" as an example here; "I stood in my own way for years, allowing my ego, "*the Whisperer"* to run and drive me literally insane with anger, rage, frustration, jealousy, envy, low self-esteem and poor personality." I am grateful to the *Creator, "The One True Master,"* that I have recognized why my life took certain turns and twists. You have the ability to live life on your terms and why not now and forever live in harmony and peace. To some of you that might mean, doing without all the toys of life. That is not true and, no one is saying that things are not important, they are! What I am saying is this; "without peace and harmony through re-creation, all the things would be a bed of chaos." Do not let appearances fool you, this is a fact of life and you do not need to study the rich and famous to find it out. Simply look in the mirror! The mirror will remind you of the need to "Re-Create," if you are totally honest with yourself. The mirror is a wonderful tool to teach us *self-reflection and introspection.* A health mind will look into the mirror and say, *"how can I improve who I am today?"* That is simply, t*hrough self or auto-suggestion,* instructing the soul, or subconscious mind to give you answers and directions on how to *"Re-Create"* you.

Catch the Whisperer Exercise

Take a sheet of paper and make a heading entitled, *"Catching the Whisperer." Make* 3 columns. The first column will be for the time. The second will be the number thought, for example; # 1. The third column will be for the thought that entered your mind. "Was it to be like someone else," or"Wishing you could be younger and do this instead of that?" Was it day dreaming of being your favorite singer or athlete or inventor? Was it getting angry about some past event, wishing you had given someone a piece of your mind in a nasty way? Was it calling a friend or a colleague to talk about your success, only to get approval and praise for your ego? Was it saying, "If it is to get done, I must do it!" There are many ways that the Whisperer can attack and the more subtle forms of attack are soft and seemingly warm with good intent. These kill and maim just as sure as the obvious ones; in fact, they are more dangerous and destructive to the self-esteem of the individual. Be sure and write the number of the thought as in the second step, and then write down what thought that you had. You will notice a pattern, but more importantly, you will be on your way to breaking the shell of the whisperer!

The Day After the (Previous) days exercise

Take another sheet of blank lined paper and again make 3 columns. The first for the thought number, the second for, "The pain avoided," and the third for, "The pleasure sought." In each column, describe the "Feeling" that you got, or that certain thought evoked. For example, one day I was thinking, "He did not have to say it to me like that, I should have told him something good, or tore him a new bottom!" The big issue here is that this is something that I obviously could not change, but my Whisperer was attempting to get me into the past and get mad about it. My ego wanted a different response, because at that moment, I was feeling embarrassed that I allowed someone to say some things to me in front of others; the whole affair bruised my "monster ego." Now, pay very close attention. When you notice this and describe how and why it made you feel a certain way, you have not only caught the enemy in his tracks, but you have exposed his very scheme! His scheme is none other than to rob you of your value. The Whisperer wants control. However, it knows that this is impossible if you are knocking fast ball, curve ball, sliders and every others pitch out of the ball park! Do these exercises for 30 days straight, and you will be amazed at the way the brain works. The Whisperer is a coward! Catch a coward and look him straight in the face and he will always retreat! The object is to know your thoughts, and control what you wish and desire to think and you can have life on your terms and not in some fantasy world made out of your own mind, with the Whisperer as your master. You must master right thinking, thereby you will learn Self-Control and then, and only then, can you have that Calmness of mind, which is power. I know from well over 40 years of experience, so if you are looking for theory, you are looking in the wrong direction.

Chapter 8 The Mind's Subconscious Rhythm

The mind of man has rhythm, and a *right spiritual* guide. Those who masterfully, and by choice, use it by commanding the most excellent that it can give, ascend just as surely as the sun rises in the two east and sets in the two west. The mind's rhythm is just as the rising or the setting sun; it rising, setting is nourishment to the soul! The mind vibrates with every other living thing, but only when peace and harmony are present. Some people harmonize to greater degrees than others, each depending on his or her own level of growth and development. That is why some people attract more abundance into their lives than others, who seemingly are just as intelligent and gifted, and even spiritually endowed. The one who vibrated at a higher level, who attracts more happiness, peace, love and prosperity, has reached a *mind* or *soul dance* level, which the other has not attained. The mind's subconscious rhythm has to be brought about deliberately as rain drops on a dry soil. Man has to put the mind in order! The Creator gave the mind *"order and proportion."* All are equal in value, and all are special and unique. Some have organized and purified the soul (subconscious) to a much greater extent than others, and that is why there is a huge difference in income, happiness, peace of mind and much more. Buddhists, Muslims, Christians and many other religions and movements chant or sing praises. These praises, songs and chants assist in bringing the mind or soul (subconscious) in harmony with the outside world. Even listening to your favorite music on the radio inspires happy thoughts and thoughts that make you want to move, groove, cry, shout, dance, laugh and just about every emotion that you can think of and feel. There are those that make some people angry. The point is this, "Chants, Praise, Music and Hymns," all create a dance in the mind or soul, (subconscious) and whether positive or negative, the mind or soul, (subconscious) will eventually receive it, because it does not distinguish between what is harmful or helpful to it. It is a wonderful servant, if you plant the right seeds; seeds of harmony, peace, love, wealth, and perfect health.

Visit www.esteemnow.com for more on programming your subconscious mind for the results you desire, for a dream fulfilling life.

Mothers often sing their babies to sleep. I use to sing or chant to my children often. In fact I witnessed the delivery process of all 4 of my children, and I promptly chanted in each of their ears this chant or praise, *"You are the greatest, I experience that there is no other greater. I experience that you are the one who communicates with the source directly as transmitter and receiver. Come to development, Come to lasting success, farming and tilling the soil of your mind, through positive thoughts for your success. You are the greatest, there is no greater than you!* These are some of the first words that my children all heard upon entering the physical world. Actually other than the doctor's words, softly spoken, these words were the very first as I stood by to take my baby as soon as

I was allowed to cut the life cord. I teach my children that, *"The Creator, or The Master" is within them, and that* they *must Awaken Him/Her and Call IT Forth!* They will then live life with the license of higher, lighter, happier beings; much like angels, but lighter and with more command, with words that are "powerful law." The purpose of teaching my children and all people the above mentioned, is to learn to *"stay in your peace."* When we do not aspire to be ourselves, we inevitably become someone else, a creation of another or an outside influence; our "ego" (temper, lust, greed, envy etc.) become "us" and "we" become lost in the "web of the ego." When we know ourselves we come into "our peace." When we come to recognize the *"Master"* in us, and obey the commands, we have power, ability and a personal magnetism beyond expression. The "ego" cannot survive in a peace and harmony evolved life, or world. Now, the ego is not bad! The ego that is allowed to run the operation of the mind is terrible and takes over the entire nervous system. The ego that is healthy says, "I am somebody of importance," I must look out for my well being and be upright and true. I must seek ways to serve humanity and respect the "self" desires and needs in "others" above my own. That is "healthy ego!" That is what Jim Rohn calls, "self-interest at the service of others, not at the expense of others."

This ego thing can be tricky and pulling the strings, for behind an unhealthy ego is the "Whisperer." My self-esteem (value) was always wrapped in what I had accomplished. Examples of accomplishments that I valued are: being number one sales person for the month or the year, or writing one of my books, or something of that nature. My self-esteem was badly abused and beaten when I did not get the recognition or get to be number one for even a short period. I had sleepless nights and much anger. I was anxious and worried about what others were doing. I maintained my number one status everywhere I had worked with maybe two exceptions. That string of success, (so called) cost me *"peace of mind and happiness."* I made enemies and caused much pain and anguish in those who did not have my drive, nor the monster ego that I had stirring inside my soul. I would seek to destroy others in the "fire" of my desire if they attempted to challenge me. That was not only being a bully but it was destroying my inner-self, as my true self suffered immensely. The façade, the mask that I had been wearing most of my life was going for the jugular vein, the life vein! The chief aim of the "Whisperer," while manipulating my ego was to get me to totally self–destruct. As I am writing this, I now know why! The reason is this, "That *Whisperer,* that voice, knows the potential in us. It knew mine better than I did, and out of desperation it was going all out to make its assault more damaging with each occurrence.

Now, pay close attention, *"the ego is not bad!"* The extreme is to think that the ego is bad and to get you to neglect your own, "healthy ego, or self-interest." That is deadly to your existence. The object of this "*Whisperer,"* is to change the *nature* of the human being. It survives off of *your* inner turmoil and conflict.

It drives you to one extreme or the other, always in an attempt to keep you *off balance*. Between the two extremes is peace of mind. In short, when this is understood and over stood, you can and will know yourself. *The people, who know who they are, can literally change themselves and change their environment.*

The Right Brain and The Left Brain

The right brain is called the *"Creative Brain,"* and the left brain is called the *"Logic or Reasoning Brain."* The right brain creates manufactures and keeps fear alive. It gives life to vain fear, created out of our imagination. It keeps it alive and protects it with a constant stream of creative garbage. The left brain then justifies the fears and makes all kinds reasons for the existence and its right to be alive. The left brain will even fight and disagree to make it's point of "justified" fear, even if it is "*The Night Of the Living Dead or The Vampire."*

The left brain also disagrees with the right or *Creative Brain,* and says, *"Stop this, stop this nonsense. You are going against our nature thereby hindering our process through life."* The *left or Logic Brain* says, *"That this is not real, the sound you heard was the floor squeaking from your own foot steps and not a so called ghost!"* It says, "*Let's reason and see what this is about. Let's find its true nature or cause."* The left brain wants to sort, calculate, reason and find solutions to the situation. For instance when someone is afraid of the *"Boogie Man"* the left brain will say, "That's baloney and you know it!" Although these fears are often picked up in our early years, people pass on this sort of garbage for generations. Even realizing this as fact, the right or *Creative Brain* comes up with more creation, distortions and mischievous, deformed creatures; with attempts to trick the *"left brain"* into going along for the ride. Many times, the left or *Logical Brain* will give up and accept the creation of the right brain. That is when fear has lodged in, and starts to do its *(sometimes or often times)* permanent damage.

Left Brain Communicating With the Right Brain

When people talk to themselves, the "*left brain*" is actually communicating with the *"right brain."* I believe that the communication goes both ways, but to keep with the point here, the *"left brain"* will ask the questions, "*How or why"* and the right brain will begin to process the question, handing it over to the soul, (subconscious mind) for the acceptance and stamp of approval. If done with faith and a true burning desire, followed by action that communicate a real desire, sooner or later the soul (subconscious) will give answers back to you with instructions and plans to carry out those instructions.. As I write, this is exactly what happened to me this morning and is happening to me at this very moment. Another way it works is like this, The "*left brain"* will make a logical or rational thought and the *"right brain"* will seek to find and connect the rational thought to a creative plan. It is only with a *"creative plan"* that any thoughts out of the left brain can come into physical existence. Thomas Edison's great work with the incandescent light and other great inventions were "left brain," scientific theories; however without the creative "right brain" faculties, the inventions would not have happened or manifested. First came the thought, "*left brain"* then the **word,** *"right brain or creation,"* then the physical manifestation. It is really simple once you think about it. The thing is to have patience with the process, and lots of it.

Right Brain Communicating with the Left Brain

The "right brain" will create, putting thoughts and things together without logic, reason or rhyme. Songs are often written with no logical flow, however they feed the soul. An artist starts to paint from somewhere within that cannot be explained, or can be best explained by calling it *"inspiration."* The word of a writer often comes from thinking, meditating, praying, singing, and driving down the street. Someone may say something that may trigger in the mind of the writer a thought that corresponds with earlier thoughts and create a masterpiece. The *"right brain"* is communicating to the *"left brain,"* let's fashion this in physical form! The "left brain" responds with, *"Who can we talk to, and what can we do to get our painting in the art galleries?" "Where can we go, what books can we read, that will get us on the road to physical manifestation?"* The "*left brain"* takes its responsibility seriously, and begins to work on the solution to the questions asked. The questions were actually communicated on a level beyond normal thought. The "*right brain*" communicated with its creativity; *(words spoken and unspoken)* the "*left brain*" asks the powerful enhancing questions, thus completing the beginning task.

They Dance and Dance

The "*left and right brains*" are performing a dance! It is first a spiritual dance, much like *Swans* do on the lake. They communicate, as everything in creation comes in pairs, The pair, (*right and left brain)* performs a *dance* like a mating dance, where the resulting thoughts, creation, logical ideas and splendid plans are the children of this great logical thinking and imaginative force. They dance to the moonlight, the sunlight, and the ocean, with and without the waves; they dance to the stars in the sky; they dance in the stars in the Eyes of male and female, male and male, female and female. In any case they dance! *They dance the greatest dance of life that most can or will ever imagine.* When you observe everything created by man, you are witnessing the dance in full view. When you see everything, "you are witnessing the *"Dance of Life."* When you witness the peace in life, and have peace and harmony in your soul, deep within you, you are experiencing, *"The Eternal Dance of Life."*

Both Right and Left Brains act as receiver and transmitter! This is truly a marvel and a generous gift from the Creator Of All Things, The One True Master that resides in you. The soul dances with itself, as it needs neither outside guidance nor influence. The soul dances like the moonlight dance across the oceans or the rivers. When we reach this level of understanding and insight, even the birds sing in harmony with us. The sun and the moon adores all, but, especially the one who does this.

Mirror Exercise

Every day, for the next 30 days, make it a point of getting in front of your mirror and asking these questions:

1. How can I improve who I am today?
2. What can I do to become the peaceful being I desire to become today? *(Assuming your aim is peace)*
3. What service can I perform today, without expecting any remuneration?" (Remember that this is not suggesting that you do not accept pay, this affirms in your soul a willingness to go the extra mile (for others) at times, without payment in the form of money.)

Think about these questions and ponder them; make them a burning desire.

Write the questions on a 3x5 Card and carry them with you. Read them at least three times daily for the first 30 days. You may read them as many times as you desire; the more you impress these questions upon your subconscious mind, the greater the effect and eventual return. *If asked in all sincerity, and with positive expectation of receiving answers and directions, one cannot help but have positive and rewarding changes in the next 30 days. If your actions are in accord with what you ask, you will feel peace, harmony and your self-esteem will start to flower. You cannot change within and feel the same without. The outer life will begin to conform to your thoughts, and this is the way we have always lived. For more information, subscribe to the ONE MINUTE ESTEEM free, two week training course. www.esteemnow.com*

Chapter 9 Whisperer of Fear

"I" is a personal pronoun. When someone says, "I fear this or that," they are actually saying, *"I am* in fear of whatever goes behind it." Fear is of your making, a manufactured entity of your own design by the "*Whisperer*" within. Your own vain imagination created it and stamped the seal of approval on it Fear may hijack you whenever it desires. That means that it has "power" over you, and you are not the commander, but the pitiful slave of your own doing. This is insane; it is insane! Yet people volunteer for induction into the *"Fear Hall of Shame."* For years I served the fear of *"The Wolf Man."* I knew that one day he would come to claim my body and rip it apart with claws and fangs. I knew that I was a wolf, ready to devour others with my vitriol and violent temper, with my fiery words and memorable infamous too letter words. For years I was a slave of my fears, until deliverance came and fear of my own making is no more. Whenever I discover old fears, they are obliterated with little or no effort on my behalf. Again, let me remind you that, "this is not some wild theory; I have lived it and have earned the integrity and the right to expound on it." You are getting genuine, heart felt information that can assist in changing your life from this moment on.

Fears Will Punish You

Your fears will punish you. They will punish you with authority, "self-ordained" authority! Your fear will fight you to stay in charge, to conquer them, you must say, "No," and face them. Someone said, "*Do The Thing You Fear And The Death Of Fear Is Certain.*" That is wise advice, which we all can learn from and live in peace and harmony. Whether you are an athlete, singer, writer, politician, clergyman, mother, father, farmer, speaker, scientist or anything or profession, *"until fear is understood at least for what it really is,"* you will not progress beyond your own prison. Until you overcome fear, you will be masquerading around being something that you know that you are really not. That is a terrible way to live and breathe. That is a burden, a self imposed burden of the worst kind. What better way to be than to be yourself?" Fear will punish you! What great things await those who can be themselves and allow serenity and peace with harmony to flow their way? What you seek is seeking you, but you do not get it because what you seek does not recognize who you say you are! What you seek in the form of material, spiritual, mental and moral, wants to shower their gifts on you, but they cannot recognize disguises and facades. Fear will punish you! *Take off the façade by releasing your fears. Tell that "Cowardly Whisperer" where to go with it. "Hit The Road and Don't Come Back No More, No More!"* That's right; talk to that Whisperer! Do not fight with a coward, just talk to it and let it know that, "*The Master Has Awakened,*" Fear is no longer a resident. Fear has been evicted! But, you must still forgive and love even then. Why? Because, "that whisperer," is a part of you." You can cause it to submit to your desired bidding and remain silent, or be useful. *Master Awaken!*

Forgiveness and Love

The Master that is within you is willing and ready to forgive you and spread the elixir of love through and through you. Forgiveness is that thing which once we learn to do and be constant at it, will give us better mental and physical health. I need not mention the "*spirit,*" because the words, "*forgiveness and love*" alone connote something "*spiritual,*" deeper than the mental and the physical. Have you forgiven your self for past pain, hurt, disappointments and setback? Have you taken the time to forgive yourself for the past mistakes and things that you did on purpose? Have you forgiven others who have done you harm or whom you have perceived to have done so? Have you forgiven your parents, siblings, cousins, and other relatives, friends and neighbors for the faults, sins and wrongs against you? If the answer is "no" to anyone of these questions, your life will be in a stalled state until you forgive from the *heart and soul.* Forgiveness releases pain, (physical, and mental) and allows the love of life the freedom to move through you. You are a vessel, a conduit, the breath of life, and the wind. *"The Spirit of The Master"* will not move upon the face of the deep, because the vision is clouded with un-forgiveness. How can one expect to *"receive"* if *"giving"* is not a law of the self? You must make giving your own personal law that you live and breathe by. It is out of this same mercy that you are able to function and move about without reprisal for past wrongs. Yet so many people receive forgiveness and never desire to give it back. Forgiveness is not the personal property of anyone. Therefore, it must be constantly given. Forgiveness is an elixir; why would you withhold something that soothes the soul, cures numerous ailments in the physical body as well as the soul? Give it and you will receive it. Withhold it and you will suffer mental, physical, emotional and every kind of anguish and pain from which human beings can and will suffer.

Not to forgive is theft; it is bullying, when the person that is un-forgiven is sorry yet, does not know that they can release themselves by self-forgiveness, and by casting away feelings of guilt.

Talking To Yourself Is Fine

The left brain talks and says to the right brain, "That's not in accord with the direction the soul, or subconscious mind, wants to go in." The left brain says, "That type of creation, (meaning fear of....) hinders our growth, prosperity and natural human propensity. " How can you have peace if you will not grow up and stop telling and believing these often childish, silly and insane lies? Yes! They are lies! Fears are lies, and half truths. Fear has to be followed by the two letter word "of." Without this "of," Fear is just a word without any pull, but the moment someone says, "Fear Of," then they have attached a thing to it; the combination of the two words, 'Fear' and 'Of' makes the false appear real. Zig Ziglar is famous for the quotation, *"FEAR is False Evidence Appearing Real."*

Chapter 10 Giving
(Keeping the Flow)

It is not the *percentage* you give that counts; what matters is "the heart, the spirit, and the reason or the intent for the giving." Whether out of a pure hearts or in developing a pure heart through demonstrating love for humanity, giving helps purify the one who gives. The motives for giving are selfish, (for ego gratification) if giving is done just to stay in good standing with your religious institution or to say, "*I tithe* every Sunday." Why do you give?

Important Exercise

Take out a sheet of paper and list the reasons you give. State what percentage of your earnings you give; (This matters least, I can assure) after you have written out why you give, you can better understand and feel better about the percentage you do give. What reaches the person, from your giving, and ultimately the "*Universe*" is not the amount or percentage. The ten percent, if that is your amount, is an idea that is good; however, it has taken the place of the reason in many instances. *Any thing you give in a spirit of perfect harmony and out of love, is a grand deposit in the Universal Bank of life and will return to you many fold.* The thought, the intent, and the heart of the matter is what "giving" is all about. I did not use the word, "*tithe*" here because that tends to cause others to think in terms of percentage, which may negate their good intent, which is rooted in the *why*.. Some people will contend that, "God said it!" I say, "Go by whatever makes you feel content." I am not trying to tell anyone how to think or how to give; I am concerned with the *spirit of giving and the reason for giving.*

Personally, I give at least ten percent of my earnings or a "Tithe." I would humbly suggest the practice of tithing to anyone who would care to listen, however, I will not contend that the percent is the magic, although some writers do; I have no basis to make the case. I do know that internally, although it has proven to be a sound system. Since there are those who tithe and are broke, just as there are those who pray and are broke, I opine that there is something deeper than the percentage given.

There is a rule or law called, *"The Law of Compensation."* The giver must receive and the receiver must give. Life will process all orders of the giver and the receiver. Life will return to you your just reward, and multiply it over and over again. This is an unfailing law; no one can escape it or cheat it. There is no such thing as something for nothing. Those who think so have doomed themselves to a life of misery and unfulfilled dreams and desires. They are afraid of their own power and peace. If you do not give or do not know how to receive, life will *"process your order"* and take away what you have! It is a great game of *"serve and be served."*

It is called, "*The Law of Service.*" Your participation in it is voluntary. However, your being affected and effected by it is not voluntary! You have the choice to play, but you have *"no choice"* in the taking or giving that it brings your way. *The Law of Service* and *The Law of Compensation* are just as essential as air. Whether you want it or not, you will breathe it or you will no longer occupy a space on this planet.

The Law of Compensation will take away from you because you took away from humanity. You attract what you are and what you put out. You put out nothing in the way of giving, therefore the law says that compensation must take place and you must pay by having something taken from you, or out of nothing. *The Universal Bank cannot be robbed!* You will pay, or give, even if it has to be extracted from you. You can choose to pay and be compensated, as is the law. Giving is not just for the needy; you can give to a worthy cause, something that will advance technology, thereby advancing life on this earth for the betterment of all. If done in sincerity, and purity of faith, that will be processed by The Universal Bank as well.

This is not, nor was it ever intended to be a discourse on the word, "tithe." However, it is and was always meant to be an awakening to what the core is, and this is, "Giving from the heart; and giving without any ulterior motive of anticipation of return. This may seem to be a "walking contradiction." I can assure you that it is not the case. The *"Law of Compensation,"* will take care of itself. Our duty is to take care of the giving, thereby releasing the *Law of Compensation,"* to work in our favor. Yes! We release that law; we can keep it flowing in our lives. We activate that law. We become one with that law, and every time we speak, do, breathe and act, we activate that law. We may as well speak now or forever hold our peace on what we wish to accomplish, because what we speak, can, shall and most definitely will be done now! It is my knowing that when we leave this body, we will get all that we did not see physically manifested in this reality. What you believe is entirely up to you, so make it a wonderful and glorious day! *Peace Be Upon You.*

Chapter 11 Don't Curse Your Crisis

Many times we look too hard at our crises and we curse them. In many ways, our crises in life are signs of growth and development. They are guide posts to a better existence, and an elixir to the mind. How many times have you had an experience from which you learned a great deal? The ordeal may have seem terrible and probably was to a certain extent, but when it was all said and done, have you ever asked yourself, *"What have I learned?"* The important thing is that you learn to turn every adversity into something beneficial for your life. The seed of greatness is in every challenge and hard time. If you are too busy "cursing" every event that does not fit into your plan, you are literally your own worst enemy. Blessings, opportunity and sunshine come in different packages.

We often ask for something and work hard to acquire it, or have great desire to achieve it, only for some of us to miss it when it comes. Do you know why? What we seek is often missed because, *"The desirer seeks to control the form and the mold that it arrives!"* The job of the one who desires and exercises creative vision is to *"see, and declare it as done."* The "*how*" is totally not the department of the seeker. The "*why*" is the job of the seeker! Make no mistake about it; many people start out correct by using the principle of self or autosuggestion, but they seek to control the conduit or the channels. *Leave that alone!* Find some business that you can mind, like thinking it, believing it, seeing it and knowing exactly what your goals are by writing them out and saying them everyday, many times per day if you are so inclined. But, do not take the class on having to *"know"* exactly *"how"* everything is going to happen. You may as well have two left feet, and constantly get in your own way. People are forever in their own way and quick to blame circumstances when man is the maker of his own circumstances, the carver of his own turkey! He often becomes the turkey!

Chapter 12 Don't Seek Validation

When validation is sought, locks (of our own manufacturing) are put on our minds. Our minds often process information that we are told or lead to believe, without investigation; we often take this information and continually tell ourselves it is fact. The sub-conscious mind eventually accepts what it is told repeatedly; at that point, you become what you were told without investigation. You live with this programming all your life, unless you break it by self or autosuggestion. Your soul (sub-conscious) demands more, clearer, brighter and more enlightenment; better understanding and soundness. I have observed many preachers, of all religions and denominations, criticize each other right in front of their entire congregation! There was a time when I would get upset and talk about it for days, however, I have come to see and learn of the great suffering that the person is enduring as demonstrated by this behavior. The soul at that point is crying out for answers. When a man is comfortable with what he believes, the need or the cause to criticize another belief system will never come up. Usually, or at least the times that I have witnessed this sort of behavior, the person speaking seemed to know little about the other way of life or its founders; that was the most astounding thing to me! I have even asked on several occasions, "Have you ever read anything about such and such way of life, or how they see God?" The answer was almost always a pathetic, "No and I do not want to know or read about that stuff!" When a man engages in such destructive and often slanderous criticism, he is not at peace in his soul with what he believes, therefore he seeks, "Amen" for his lack of Self-Esteem.

When someone asks another, "what religion are you?" They are seeking validation for what they believe to be the right religion, and their soul is crying for help! I told one gentleman, "If you have to ask, you have not arrived." Those who do this, seek to be released from narrow mindedness, petty distinctions and prejudices of all kinds. People imprison their soul, (sub-conscious mind) by narrow mindedness and refusal to search for the hidden jewels within. Most people are afraid, (I believe) to ask God, "Is this the truth?" "Is what I believe the whole truth or is there more to my existence?" FEAR! Fear is the reason that most people will never ask this question; they are afraid that they will get in trouble with God by asking questions. Actually, they are not afraid of "God," they are afraid of their own great potential and will to succeed at any worth while undertaking. When we take in information as children, we are not responsible. However, once we become able adults, we shoulder the responsibility to think. Yes, Think! That inner voice, (*The Whisperer*) will suggest to you that you are ungrateful and not a good servant if you ask questions, when it does, you just have to say, "Shut up and get in line!" Believe me, if you do this, the chatter will stop. I have done this on many occasions. I use to allow my inner voice, *(The Whisperer)* to have its way and before I knew it, I was in a rage and ready to take some action, usually the wrong action. When I learned to silence the rebel, it worked like a charm. Until you learn to do this as often as needed, you will continue to be assaulted from within. You will never have the courage to ask the empowering questions and your soul, (sub-conscious mind) cannot answer what you do not ask it. Now, there are outside, or suggestions from others that can and will influence you, make no mistake about it. But, tell me, "*Would you rather influence your own mind with healthy, harmonious, peace loving and wealthy building thoughts, or let some outside influence take this job?*" I know the answer that is right for me; I will let you make the decision for yourself of what is best or right for you..

Now, I understand that family members and friends will call you crazy, and blasphemous for questioning your beliefs, (not just religious) but it is my humble opinion, "It is blasphemous and treacherous to the sub-conscious and the total self, not to question and investigate what you are told and have been taught all of your life." It is much easier and less work to be a sheep, or cow; being lead off a cliff or to the slaughter house. Why, *"because everyone else does it therefore it must be the right thing to do."* That is called, *"crowd"* mentality and when you do that, you have given up all self-identity.

Do you know that you give up your freedom *(the most valuable thing on earth)* when you behave in this manner? You are free to think for yourself. Those who suggest that you are a rebel, or some sort of evil person are themselves blind, or manipulative or both! Here is one really sound thought, something that I suggest that everyone reading this should think about for about thirty minutes, early in the morning before most are awake. Think about this, "Most of what we believe is not written or confirmed by us, why? " Why you have not gone into whatever it is that you have been taught, or told all of your life and checked its soundness, and asked God in prayer for clarity? Why do you believe, (if you do) that your way is the only way, and that all others are doomed?" I have an answer, but still do the exercise and write down you answers. Here is a thought which is my answer; *"Most people have low Self-Esteem!"* The self value is low, therefore anything, any click or gang or group thought that will give the human being a sense of value will be accepted as the whole truth and nothing but the truth. Any thought to the contrary will be ridiculed and mocked. Most people will never investigate a thing that they are raised to believe or that the crowd believes. *Self-Esteem means or signifies that you are comfortable with the mind that you have and, its ability to solve problems lead you to viable solutions, lead to the right people, places and things, for the right answers, at the right time and in the right way.* Self-esteem is the building block for healthy self-confidence. When you understand that you have patency, that you have a divine purpose which no one is to fill but you, you attain, "true self-confidence." Your life is no longer in the hands of someone else, who may have had something in mind other than what you aspire to live. Self-esteem builds and leads to courage and fortitude. Courage is inner and your courage will stand up and say, "Let's check this out." That is your duty and your price for having passed through this life. If you accept this, and live it; *"The Master No Longer Reclines, He Has Awakened Within You and It Will Guide You!"* The doors that will open for you will make your heart dance with joy. Your thoughts will guide you to riches within you that you never knew could exist in one person. Once you understand and accept your Self-esteem is your value self, you will understand that you have been successful all the time. *You are just as successful as anyone on the planet. I mean what I just said in a literal way. I am not being philosophical at all! "The Source" (which is you) gave you the best value, which means that you are as successful right now as anyone. You no longer have to just accept anything without your value system seeking some understanding and insight.*

If you just sit there and are a receptacle for any and all ideas and thoughts outside of yourself, you are in a vegetation state; all you require is a little sunlight and water and tender care and you will be just fine. "Many of you do not require much at this point, because you do not want to *become* much." The plant is better off than you for this reason; the plant has no higher form, and therefore it is perfect. You, on the other hand are living *below your potential* and doing a great injustice to the great mind and body with which God blessed you.

Chapter 13 The Happy You!

"If you want to be happy, set a goal that commands your thoughts, liberates your energy, and inspires your hopes." **Andrew Carnegie**

For years I sought happiness outside of me, wanting to impress others with my achievements and my determination to set my mind on a thing and achieve it. I sought other peoples' approval more than I recognized the value and strength that "The Creator" had given my soul. I lived this way for nearly 40 years of my life. I was not happy, nor was I peaceful and I did not have harmony. Anything that someone else said that did not agree with my feelings or thoughts, would get my immediately rebuke or even verbal assault. I would allow what others thought of me to burn in my mind and heart for days, weeks and sometimes months. Some of the self-inflicted scars lasted for years. What I later discovered was that, the key to this type of self-hatred is unhappiness with self. I thought for years that once I achieved this or that, the world would accept me, and then I would be happy and successful. I learned that the more I attempted to do just that, the angrier, unhappier and disharmonious I became in my soul.

I sought for years what was already mine by divine right. I set goals and would go after them with the tenacity of a bull dog! I would have focus and determination, but for what? It was really to seek approval of my self-worth! My self-esteem took a tremendous beating every time. Every attempt at pleasing someone else and looking for the value in me with others approval shattered my self-esteem. I had no idea that all this was ever taking place. I spent time in jail. I studied as much or more than a 4 year Harvard or Yale graduate, and yet I never looked for the meaning of the word *"Self-Esteem."* Let me make this perfectly clear, *"I am a student of language, words, and expression!"* I am also a student of one of the finest vocabulary programs put together by, Charles H. Elster titled ***"Verbal Advantage."***

I am not bragging, but, "I am no second banana" when it comes to studying and learning and applying words and phrases. I love great inspiring quotes. Why had I never, until November 2004, added the word, *"Self-esteem"* to my vocabulary and daily affirmations? This is/was puzzling to me in light of what I would come to learn of the word, "Self-esteem." I then looked up the word and saw that it means "self-value." I casually added it to my vocabulary because it sounded good and it seemed to fit my expressions. I now understand that nothing happens by chance. I would later discover that I was destined to find true happiness and there can be no true happiness without having a healthy *"Self-esteem."* My life had suffered by my own hands, and happiness had so far evaded me because I had been rejecting it. I had not recognized that happiness is not things, not love, not fine cars or nice homes, not women nor song nor anything else for which you yearn. Instead, being happy is what it is. "Happiness is Happiness." When I learned to love myself and appreciate what "The Creator" had given me, I began to understand that "I

Am!" and that, "I Am Happy Now!" I love me and you must love you now, today and forever; no amount of shuffle, jiving and conniving to convince or please others will bring happiness. Wally Famous Amos is quoted as saying, *"Happiness is an inside job."* No one can ever rival me, I am the greatest creation ever created! No amount of fame, fortune and wealth can add to the great, marvelous and wonderful value that I already have, because the Creator made me special. I am a jewel, a diamond, and pure sunshine radiates from my heart and soul. I am happy because of who I am now, not "when" but now and that is the way my life is supposed to be and always will be. I tell myself that I am Happy, Happy, Happy and peaceful every single day. Tell yourself that your happiness does not depend on things, other people, or their approval, nor on your skin color, your house or car, or the amount, or size of your bank account! Your happiness is decided by you, when you decide to appreciate that *"You are the most special thing The Creator has ever created."* You are second to none and inimitable when compared to all. No one will ever think, see, and dream quite like you. No one will ever sing the song like you, or write the books you write like you, or design the clothing that you will design. Be happy with you and you will have discovered what jewel or rarity that you really are. You do not have to "Try" to be anything, because nothing is like you! Everything is here to serve you and your gift to the Creator is to serve it back to show your sincere appreciation. It is only through sharing and giving back, that we can show our appreciation for the gift of being one of a kind. Do not be shallow and underestimate your self-worth. When you do, you deprive the world of the greatest someone that has ever set foot on the planet and in the universe. *The Creator Makes No Mistakes. He Only Makes The Best of The Best In The Most Excellent Form.* Tell yourself this every day, and you will begin to feel and believe how important you are, and, as a result, you must become a happier you.

Failures (Temporary Defeats)

I have had countless set backs and temporary defeats that I would later understand were not failures. They were guide posts in my journey to be really happy with who and what I am. I would self-destruct the moment I saw success coming to me, I would fail! This sounds strange, but I believe it to be the story for a great number of people. Had you told me that I feared success, as I did, I would have referred you to the fruit farm! I really did fear success because true success is peace and happiness. I had none of it! I have had many promising positions. I have been top salesman many times. For many months, the *"so called"* competition in the office, would give up after the third month or so of any thought of catching me, until some *fresh meat* would be hired and I would take care of them also. This all felt good, however I was hiding something deep and hurting, I was seeking happiness by approval and at the same time I was becoming arrogant and disrespectful to those around me. I became bigger than the owners in their own company. In case you have not heard, "no one wants to deal with a spoiled disrespectful employee," especially if they have gone out of their way to make things comfortable for them and pay them well at that! Eventually, when my employers would no longer tolerate my egotistic, arrogant and reprehensible attitude, they did what most people would do, they found a reason, or in some cases created a reason, to terminate my position. All of them, (there were about 7-10) admitted this one fact at least, "Tamir is a top or the top performer, and a good worker." When asked why they had terminated me, they all had reasons that did not make any sense for business or personal reasons. If they had told the real reason, I believe that they were afraid that they would have had to pay large sums of money. However, why should anyone have to put up with an inharmonious, ungrateful, individual who knows nothing but what he wants? I did more work than I was paid for. This was/is a tremendous asset to anyone, any employee and any employer. No one in their right mind would terminate a relationship were the employee always arrived early and left late; would sell with the ease and comfort of a master and would get referrals at will! I was a company man in every job, yet I found ways to self-destruct.

I would leave making excuses, file legal action and talk about how bad they did me because they were intimidated by me. I thought that they all were jealous and thought that I would eventually have their jobs. That was insane; i could not figure it out. How could someone hire me and then, because I make them a ton of money fire me because they were jealous, racist or what have you? Here is the irony of it all; I even accused another man of color of the same thing. I accused him of favoring the other employees over me because I was not of the same ethnic group. The other employees were East Indian. When I was fired, I was thinking, "I failed again." This was another "temporary setback," that I mislabeled "failure." When it all boiled downed, I was my own worst enemy. At the same time, I was gaining a lesson that would be worth more than anyone could come up with; monetary or otherwise. These experiences were stumbling blocks and nothing more! They were there to serve me and to instruct me in human nature, empathy and a profound appreciation for each day and each opportunity that each day brings. I learned that, *"no one owed me anything,* that I made my own success, and fueled my own failures. I eventually learned, that *"I am the master of my life and the captain of my soul." Everyone else is just a player in the script, and so it is with every human being.* If i do not determine what goes on in my life, who will?

See It In The Best Light!

Mixed with all the stuff, was the right stuff: the enthusiasm, drive, concentration, determination and the habit of doing much more than I was paid for; the defined purpose, backed by action, action and more action; backed by and mixed with my anger, fears, doubt, and lack of self-esteem. These were coupled with a caring, loving, sensitive individual with a pleasing personality, and sales skills that most would praise and gladly hire or have on their team. Mixed with the fore going were all the trials and ups and downs and hardships, bankruptcy, foreclosures, and light and water disconnected. In the face of all this was a man who prayed to the Creator of all things, several times each day; a man who read, listened to tapes, cassette disks and searched for answers in his soul. Most of my searching was for outer expression, until the last year before I would come to the most powerful realization of my life. It was around October 2004 that my focus began to shift and my soul stood up and pushed to be free. It is as if a voice inside of me commanded me, *"Awaken!"* The battle of the "child" in me versus the concocted, facade that I had become, had entered into the last round; I knew that I would either be made or be broken at that point. In the end, the victory would belong to *Gary*, the "child" inside of me. I became an *Awakened* man that day in February 2005; the master had indeed awakened! The battle was not mine, but that of "*The Creator of all things."* Many times we take on burdens that we cannot bear, and we must learn to surrender, and in all our ways and dealings acknowledge "The Creator;" the one true master of the universe and everything in it!

The skills, talents, persistence and creative expressions that stirred my soul were fueled by the breath of life, and fashioned by the *"Mighty Hand of The Creator!"* The low self-esteem, the anger, envy, false pride, doubt and misguided ego where all machinations of my imagination lead by the *"Wiley Whisperer!"* That same "Whisperer" would always run and hide after the deed; after dropping poison into the hearts of those victims that would permit such.

We all have such inner battles. We all have some sort of issue to resolve; I have come to realize that these things that I have described in this entire book are not mine solely! Every single person on the planet that reaches the age of puberty or before perhaps, have to go through the fire to burn off the waste to get to the diamond inside. My experiences have thoroughly convinced me and given me the license, the wisdom, and the under-standing of human nature that no amount of money could ever buy! I see humanity in a different light, a light that shines brighter. All of our struggles are for the good! Everything works for the good; everything happens for a reason and a season. It is this attitude of understanding that will take you through the storm of life to the beaches of paradise. The paradise in the mind is where you will find happiness, peace, and harmony; it is within your soul! You will find your dreams have been waiting for you and that they were guiding you all the time. Your dreams and hopes are you! They were always willing to lend a helping hand or give a needed suggestion. As long as you were willing to ask, and follow the way. You were never alone, never in the dark; you just had blind folds over your eyes. Time is not an issue except in the eyes of man. Time plays no favorite and will not do any disservice to anyone. It is often *"we,"* who do the disservice to the great gift of time.

"Happiness lies in the future, never in the past. The happy person is the one who dreams of heights of achievement that are yet attained." **Napoleon Hill**

"The Sign of a Healthy Person Is To Look In the Mirror, And See All That Is Right Instead of All That Is Wrong"

I came to a point where I began to entertain thoughts of doubt; some of the old fears tried to come back. I had been in a state of total bliss for the first 4 weeks following the realization of who I am and my value as a human being. Now I was starting to wonder, *"What do I do now, and how do I proceed?"* I was deep in thought when a close friend said to me, *"You have the tools, and all you have to do now is take action."* I asked, "What about the thoughts, the blissful feelings, the inspiration and creativity that embraced my soul and flowed so easily the last 4 weeks?" He said, *"It is all still there! You just have to act now and more will come. You must work with what you have, and more will come. More can do you no good if you have not worked on what you have."*

I realized then, that I have to let it flow and I would surely grow! I also remembered the great stories that I had read in the past of the lives of great men and women; *"They all had similar experiences with their own success."* I believe that such thoughts, doubts and fears are necessary to assist in our further development. I did not want to have doubt nor fear, therefore I demanded that I conquer these two enemies of the true self. I had to become comfortable with the discovery of my true self. The old doubts and fears of years of mental conditioning do not want to die, but *"die they must, die they will, die they have!"* The fear of success is behind of all this kind of fear. The fear of success is tricky and the most cunning in this writers opinion. I never knew that anything as such could be a part of me. I would affirm, *"I am confident, talented and bold"* I had to succeed sooner or later, and I did succeed! I succeeded after I realized that *success* is *a journey, a process* and not a destination. You can only succeed by going through the process. The process is success! Success is a journey, the journey is the process. I am and you are successful now; if you accept it and know it! Everyday that you set out on the journey to accomplish your goals, you are successful, one day at a time. Let no one ever tell you differently. You can be as successful as anyone on the planet, past, present and future if you grasp what you just read. Above all, when you acquire peace of mind and harmony, you will not have to think of whether you are successful or not. You will know it with certainty of mind and heart. Others will see it and you will shine with confidence and a healthy self-esteem.

Success will not allow you to be disorganized or chaotic. Success is an inside job! Success, peace of mind and harmony can only flourish in an organized environment. Organization is respecting our conscious, because your conscious will tell you what it needs to be healthy. Your living space, your car and every part of your life will flow much smoother with organization; it is the natural order of things. Once you organize your life, you will find it much easier to conquer all doubts and fears. Once you do, you will open the gate of your hearts desires.

To download a copy of "The Happy You," visit www.esteemnow.com

Chapter 14 On The One!

Everything is connected, on the one! Everything that happens that grows or shines or cries or laughs, sing, dance and play, serves a purpose in your life. Every ant that crawls, where it crawls, every bee that stings and in every drop of rain there is some lesson, some wisdom to be learned for your advancement in life. Everything in life serves to serve you! All accidents, all animals, all thoughts, dreams and visions, all sounds and colors in the rainbow serve to assist you in your life purpose. Everything imaginable and unimaginable past present and future serves to assist you in your life journey to success. Every act of "The Creator," every movement of his mighty hand and his breath of life is for your development and growth. Every lesson learned, unlearned and to be learned is for your edification, past, present and future. Every child that is born, was born, and will be born, every act of love; kindness and compassion are a sign and a lesson for your personal growth. Everything happens for you! There is not an insect that creeps in the darkness of night in the darkest of the most remote place on earth that moves, that is not for your growth and success. All things are, "On the One!" Every fish that swims in the deepest part of the deepest ocean and those that are eaten by the larger fish are all serving a purpose for your growth and success. Every scientific discovery, every new development in the material world is to serve you. I am talking about you individually! Yes, You! Don't look around and say, "Well he is talking about everyone else?" No, "I am talking about you and you alone!" Every thought seed, weed, apple tree and vegetable garden is for your learning, growth and revival. Every child born is you and you are every child born now and for all eternity! Every time a mother chastises her child, you are also being chastised; every sting of the slave master's whip is your sting, and every victim of violence is you! You are the world and the world is you; when you smile, the world smiles, when you frown, the world will frown. When a father is mean and harsh to his wife, family and friends, he is harsh and mean to you. When a great thinker, (like Ben Franklin) is set loose on the planet, you too are set loose. When a moral is perverted and corrupt, your moral is perverted and corrupt. When one child is hungry, you are hungry and when you are fed, the child is fed. *Bless the children! Bless the children! Bless the children!* They are you and you are them. What are you but what you were when you were born except an older you? Bless the children! Every sentence of death is your sentence and every wedding is your wedding. Every animal and plant is you and you are them in another form. Every star in the sky and every chirp of birds is an instruction for you and your journey through this life. Every word ever written and every word ever spoken, thought of or whispered is about you and for your benefit and edification. Every church, mosque, synagogue, temple and school is for you. Every graduation is your graduation and every sincere gift given is given by you, to you. Every mother is your mother and every father is your father. My neighbor's yard is my yard, and my neighbor's beautiful cars, boats and even his money is my mine.

Every lying treacherous person is you and every gentle, peace loving honest truth seeker is you too! We are all connected and this we cannot escape; but, why should we desire too? With everything in life there is a pair. All things are created in pairs. Human beings who have become criminals are honest descent citizens, who made adverse choices. That same man, once he makes prudent upright decisions, will attract excellent situations to himself. Out of darkness comes the light and the light is rolled into the darkness. There is sunshine and rain, fire and ice, happy and sad, eat or be eaten! Life is not complex, but it is so, only in the minds of those who have not come to understand the great laws that govern life.

The angry person is soft and calm, the calm man is the angry man matured in his soul. The unhappy person is the happy person who has lost purpose. *Serve humanity, serve humanity,* and constantly *serve humanity* and you will be serving yourself by doing so. Every victory in life is yours and every defeat you must meet with enthusiasm because your success depends on the very thing we call "failure." Someone said, *"To succeed, fail, but double your failure rate!"* The poor and the rich are the same, if you do not believe it, go to any public place and notice who goes to the rest room! Billionaires have bathrooms too in their homes; if they do not have peace of mind, their lives will be just as miserable as yours if you do not have peace of mind. Get Peace Of Mind Now! The thing man runs from, he finds wherever he stops running! If he runs into the hands of the police after being chased by criminals, he ran right into the arms of the worst criminal. If he runs to his mother or brother, he runs to a more empathetic criminal, but of a more gentle nature perhaps! The criminal element is within and must be uprooted and then one can be free. When a man goes fishing, he fishes for himself; he catches none other than himself and he fillets and cuts and eats himself. When one finds a diamond or discovers gold, he only discovered what is within. When one discovers and finds that which he does not desire, he finds in himself, that which is undesirable. When the weather is nice outside, the weather is nice inside, when the weather is inclement; the inside is stormy, dusty, tempestuous and rocky. When heaven shines down on earth, heaven shines in the heart and hell fury is wide spread. Why would heaven have significance if there was nothing to contrast it with? Hell too, is a necessary thing; without which the promise of heaven would be of no importance. The riches you seek, seek you also, the poverty you avoid, meets you at every turn and blow of the wind. The love you give, you will receive. The hate that you send out boomerangs back to you! The soil that the farmer tills is the soil of his being, his very soul. The thought you think will determine what you drink. What you ask will come to past, and that on which you knock, will open to you. Knock on the neighbor's door and see if they open it or answer your call! If they do not open the door or answer your call, you must go from house to house and door to door; and sooner or later someone will answer. This is the great law that Jesus, *"The Christ"* gave. You cannot ask and not receive, you cannot seek and not find; you must not give up, or you will never understand the great *law of attraction*. What you do to others, is done to you. That is called the *"Law of Cause and Effect"* or better known as *"The Golden Rule."* You cannot *"be or become"* and not have, and you cannot have and have not *"become,"* that would be impossible. You cannot reap where you have not sown; you cannot sow unless you reap first! You must reap the seed of the thought in your mind before you can sow the action! You cannot grow unless you learn a lesson; you will not learn a lesson until you grow. The hair that is gray is yours and the folly of the youth is your child too. You are a reaper and a sower, and whatever you reap you will sow! You are no more than a sender and a receiver and what you send you receive, and what you receive, you send out. When it rains in Africa, it rains on you, no matter where you are. When a wild animal is hunted and killed for ego and to make a trophy, man has killed himself and hung himself and his fellow man as a trophy. When the soil is tilled and the seeds are planted, so are the seeds planted in the hearts and minds of all humanity. When Thomas Edison made his many great discoveries, you celebrated too; or should have! Why not celebrate now? Are you surprised or impressed by what I write? I exhort you, "Do not be surprised or impressed!" These things are all your thoughts and my fingers are writing your words. What you may call creativity is your creativity being expressed outside of you, but it is you! The song that you love so much, and the dance that you love, are your creation and your master pieces. If this were not true, you would not be able to relate to the music and the dance steps, you would totally ignore each. We rush to quote the sages of old in saying, "I am learned, look at me!" In reality, they are you and you are the sage of times gone by and times to come. *Envy and jealousy are indeed naivety and ignorance,* as the immortal Emerson once wrote:

"We are the star that shines, and we are the ocean tides. We look for the silver lining outside, while inside it radiates with splendor! We must recognize that which we are; we are more than just a bundle of wavering thoughts and machinations of the mind. The ghost and living dead that you fear, is you and you are them."

The accident you fear or dread is waiting for you to express it in the physical reality. You are powerful beyond measure and that is why so many are afraid of themselves. Closing doors and locking windows will not save you, for every sleeping or waking hour, what you fear is with you, because, "it is you!" Your fears are one with you and one with the world! When man is afraid, mankind is afraid. You are humanity, and humanity is you.

We are one, The Creation is one. We have the unique ability to choose "which" one we want to be! If you leave it to fate, I guarantee, the choice that fate makes will not be favorable. Why should fate hand you something good, like peace of mind, when you did not ask, seek, nor knock? Fate too, is bound by the universal laws of life. Fate has no power but the power to deliver what we ask for by our thoughts, inactions or actions.

Luck? I have never seen nor heard luck; this is one evasive fellow! When you find him, bind him, and then grind him until he exposes his influence, methods and techniques on so many people, who believe in his fairy tale existence. The only luck that would exist is that which we create by our thoughts, actions and more of the same. Even a bounce is not lucky! The ball will bounce according to its created nature, but mainly because of the laws governing that nature. There is not luck in it! Try telling the people that extracted the material for the rubber out of the earth and did all that was done to make a ball that will bounce that "luck" made the ball bounce a certain way. When the ball bounces, you too bounce and when the batter hits a grand slam, you hit a grand slam; you are the ball, the batter and the bat! Put up one finger and look in the mirror and say, *"We are people, one creation with one destiny. We are all human."* That destiny is peace of heart, mind, body and soul. If you can do this with all honesty, I would love to see you run for public office in any state, city or county in the world! I am not being facetious; on the contrary, I am serious! All who can state the above would be a better public official than one who could not or would not say it.

The next person, thing or thought you see or think about, think this, *"I salute the Creator within you,"* I wish you peace all the days of your life and more. I see your kindness and loving soul, I pray for your success, as much as you desire. Say, "*I am not an enemy to anyone, but everyone is my friend. The enemy of anyone is an enemy to me, but I am not an enemy to anyone, not even the enemy of me.*" The enemy's thoughts and ways to him; are my thoughts and ways to me. Why should I allow such thoughts to occupy space in my mind where peace lives and will spread all the days of my life? Enemies are born of fear! It has been said that, *"Man is God afraid."* What do we really have to fear but our own machinations and mental torture? There is nothing that the man cannot achieve once all fear and doubts are conquered and overcome. Be bold with whatever you fear; when it shows up in whatever form, say to it, *"shut up and go to some nothing resting place!"* I have said many times to fears, *"Silence, before I decide not to turn you into an asset, or employ the alternative, and make you disappear altogether."* Then I would say, *"Get in line, it is time to pray."* Yes! I really did take it that far with my self talk! My aunt said to me one day, *"I asked myself one morning, when are you going to control your thoughts and stop allowing your thoughts to control you?"* That, to me, was a powerful simple statement that everyone might consider making. That question caused me to start thinking about my own mind; if in fact I was the master or was it was controlling me? The mind is the only thing which we as human beings have complete control over. It is a shame that most of us never take this great asset, and utilize it for the development of the quality of life that we desire.

Balance (The Middle Course)

If someone were to ask me, "What is the one thing you would say that is most important in healthy self-esteem building?" I would tell them without batting an eye, *"Keeping balance in all things!"* Let us start with you! You are not perfect in your flesh and pressuring yourself to live up to someone else's expectations cripples your creativity. You will make mistakes, but being too down on *"you"* is unhealthy, and is in itself the workings of an unhealthy self-esteem. It is natural, warm and empathetic to show concern when your performance is not up to your expectations, or that of your parents, spouse or even your children. In fact, a healthy self-reflection is one of the keys, which will keep you in balance. To ensure this, you must learn to forgive yourself and others and not make of the situation more than what it is. Having a balanced perspective on things is the state of bliss that most desire to live in. Atrophy will set in as sure as sin, if you were to be unforgiving to yourself and others for past mistakes, wrong doings and things beyond your immediate control. Eventually, after enough beating and demoralizing yourself, you will become accustomed to this torture, and believe it or not, you will do things that bring about failure and unhappiness. That is a form of atrophy! Not using the great potential in us is akin to decay; it is decay! Using your mind in any way other than for the betterment of self, through service and the uplifting of others is detrimental to your entire existence. The answer is balance; a healthy self-esteem requires balance and compassion. You must not only allow yourself room for mistakes, you must also allow room for the mistakes of others. Reframing your thoughts and situations are another form of balance. Say for instance someone cuts you off in traffic and then gives you the middle finger and yells a four letter word at you, you can reframe the incident and say, "He must have a pressing concern that must be dealt with." But, say it and mean it as if it is the actual case, whether you know it to be or not. This is not lying to yourself; you are giving a fellow human being the benefit of the doubt. You are giving yourself and your subconscious mind a moral boost. The act of balancing requires that you see the good in every situation as far as your understanding will allow. Compassion is showing empathy and consideration as to why things may happen. The first response, that I used to have, was to give the finger back and blow my horn until the person acknowledged me. After careful thought and a little assistance from hearing of all the freeway rampages, "I thought it to be a better policy to be more compassionate and forgiving." Anger is about being out of balance. That is all anger is. Anger is a form of insanity, insanity from being out of balance, (harmony) with the natural order of the soul or self. Now, let us not confuse righteous indignation with blind fury and rage, there is a difference. Aristotle said it best thousands of years ago when he wrote, "*Anyone can become angry, that is easy. But to be angry with the right person, to the right degree, at the right time, for the right purpose, and in the right way, that is not easy.*" Yes, he was speaking of having balance in emotion, feelings and gut instinct. It takes balance more than anything else to understand deeply what Aristotle said or wrote centuries ago. To have balance our emotions must be educated to know when, what, where, how and why! *When to forgive, whom to forgive, how to forgive, where to forgive, what to forgive and most importantly, "Why We Forgive!"* You cannot forgive because it is fashionable or a fad. Your forgiveness must come from a balanced healthy state, deep inside of you.

The safest course for human beings as far as love, justice, happiness, truth and peace of mind are concerned is that which comes out of balance. When balance is absent, small, big and enormous injustices are done to humanity. Adolph Hitler is an individual who come to mind immediately when imbalance comes to view. That man had an imbalance in his subconscious! I am not saying how it got there, however, I can say with certainty and with no medical diagnosis to prove it, that "Hitler had deadly issues," and I doubt that anyone would disagree, barring a few others who undoubtedly have some deep issues themselves. This case is the extreme and the world will no longer tolerate any such behavior on that scale. That is great, but it does not negate the need to teach balance, empathy and compassion to our children who are our future and always will be. Hitler was once someone's child also! What went wrong in his conscious and sub-conscious mind? While I am not an expert on Hitler, I would say without flinching that it started very early in his life, and in past lives. That is where we must start with future generations today, now! Teach balance at the tender age of 0 to 5 years of age and show it by your actions and deeds; you will have blessed the world. Neglect to do this and you are playing roulette with the lives in the world!

Look at people who are in jails, prisons and institutions of all kinds because of some act they committed over a love affair! Many of these crimes against others are committed because of *"fear of rejection, fear of being alone, fear of criticism and fear of self!"* These individuals lack balance. They do not love themselves enough. That is a major issue, and one that deserves more than just a fleeting thought. When love of self is healthy and your self-esteem is strong, things hurt; pain of an emotional nature will be felt. However, the individual with a healthy love for self and strong self-value *(self-esteem)* will more than weather the storms and tides of emotions. That is the balance that I am talking about. Balance will allow you to rise above the emotion and see things from an onlooker's perspective. When a situation can be looked at from an "*overview,"* rather than an *"under view,* or in *the view"* it can be seen as what it really is! It is never what we make it out to be when we are in a state of emotional turmoil, or imbalance. This is not some self-serving garbage thrown together to make good reading, this is serious. If you doubt for one instant the seriousness of the subject of having balance, emotional balance as well as other forms of balance, just look at and visit any state prison system! Visit the mental hospitals and orphanages, and half-way houses, or take time to attend an AA meeting or two! What do you consider spousal abuse is all about? How about drunk driving? These are all emotional issues, rooted in imbalance in the inner self! Therefore, the answer and the cure must come from within; those who are balanced must assist those who are trapped. Besides, they, (*The Emotionally Imbalanced)* and you are the same! If one person is sick, all are affected, and when one is healthy, health radiates to all. Go to the chapter, *"On the One"* (even if you have already read it) and refresh your mind on some of the concepts there, before reading any further. Balance to the life of an individual is what wheels are to a car! Balance gives you the ability to move about and function smoothly with purpose. When balance is present, the opportunities you seek will seek you because of the great universal law of balance. Balance and Order and Proportion are closely related if not one and the same coin. In order to have order, you must have balance, and for balance, there must be order. Balance is made to order! Order and proportion are derived out of balance and there is no escaping this fact.

Balance is another way or form of having self-control! *Mix self-control with enthusiasm* for life and its splendid opportunities, and you will attract more of those same splendid opportunities to you. The balance that we seek through self-control and healthy enthusiasm is the foundation that a life full of peace and love will advance towards.

I have long been a person of great enthusiasm, but without the self-control. There have been times when

I would allow my emotions to take me on an emotional whirl wind and back! Each incident, each time, my self-esteem took a tremendous pounding; my soul knew that an explosive temper and talking too much was destructive. Each incident would confirm the fact that I had little or no self-control. No self-control, no balance! It is as simple as that. I could never achieve the success that I sought without balance, which results from self-control. More importantly, *I knew that I would never know and understand peace of mind which can only be acquired through self-control, and a balanced mind, with a healthy enthusiasm for life.* I desired calmness, peace, right thought and self mastery so intensely that I attracted the right books, tapes, and people to my reality that lead me to the study of those subjects and to a life devoted to balance through self-control, and a healthy enthusiasm for life and people. I have found my self-esteem in my self, therefore balance. Balance will only come when the self-esteem is healthy; self-control and a healthy enthusiasm are the foundation of balance. Of all these, self-control, enthusiasm and self-esteem, Self-esteem is the most important. It is the natural building block of a healthy mind. Without a healthy, strong self-esteem, self-control is not possible. Just think; "How can you have self-control if you do not know and appreciate your true value?" That is what self-esteem is! Because of the three, self-control, self-esteem and enthusiasm, enthusiasm is the one that can easily cause one to become over zealous and employ caustic actions, thereby turning others away and attracting the same to your self. Remember that, "self-esteem is the main focus of this entire book!" I would not be surprised by now if you have not purchased at least three different books on the subject of self-esteem after reading the first twenty five or so pages of this book.

Chapter 15 Self-Control
(Controlling What You Think)

Self-control is thought control, so how much of it can you have if you do all the talking? Can someone else get a word in sometimes? If this is you, then the next few paragraphs may be of keen interest to you and your life.

Bravo for those of us who have enough self-control to guard our tongues! I had the damaging habit of *talking too* much and taking control of the conversation whenever I could. I had to show my superior communication skills and knowledge of words to everyone that would listen. Did you notice that I said, *"Superior communication skills?"* That is an oxymoron, if ever there was one! Superior skills in communication require that you listen far more than you speak. I exercised so little self-control that those who were weak themselves would constantly seek me out for verbal and oral beatings, while those who wanted a chance to speak themselves would rarely come around. I had gotten so good with talking that I was able to listen just long enough to allow me to get my say in, and then surgically insert my egotistically crafted admonitions, rebukes, and compliments along with my verbose narrative, into the conversation. That was *lack of self-control!* The sad thing about it was that "I had no clue as to what I was doing." I learned that words were powerful and that my use of them was great. I believed that those who did not like to here me speak were jealous because they did not have the skill nor the talent. The Inner Whisperer had really done a job on me and I did not even suspect anything to be wrong or out of place. I have learned that one of life's most valuable lessons could only be learned by listening and careful observation. One of life's most valuable lessons is this, "*People want to feel appreciated and important.*" How can you make people feel important and appreciated if you are doing all of the talking? Talking too much not only shows the world that you lack self-control; it also says that you lack the sensitivity for the needs of others. This is all unconscious and most people never realize it. When I realized that I was damaging my own self worth by not listening to others and having to say the first, middle and last words, I did some serious soul searching and found that my peace of mind was directly related to how I related to others. When I communicate with others now, I do just that, *"I communicate."* I listen and ask questions, show interest in what others have to say. You can feel the effect that this type of communication has on others. I have had many people say to me, *"you are a good man. I trust you and I can be totally open with you."* These are people that I may have met only minutes before! All I did was *ask questions, be polite in doing so, smile, make warm eye contact and listen with the intent of learning and building rapport.* This is always done with the utmost sincerity and deep interest in the other person. Everybody is important! Before I learned this lesson, I did not make others feel this way. My *lack of self-control* was dominating others, but worse, it was dominating me and hindering my progress. I used talking to conceal something deeper. That something deeper was *low of self-*

esteem. Remember that this was all done subconsciously. I do not think that anyone would purposely and maliciously damage their own self-esteem and take all prisoners with them. In closing this session on "talking too much" I would like to add, that speech is a great tool, if used in the right way, for the right reason, at the right time and for the right cause. Remember this, "Every word you speak impresses your subconscious mind, which is power without direction!" Imagine that as you go about your day and meet and greet others. Every good you speak comes to impress upon your subconscious mind and in like manner, so does every bad or ill. Knowing this truth, you can now understand why our circumstances are justly ordered and justly delivered by ourselves.

Laughter

Laughter is good and can be therapeutic. Laughter can make your day brighter and lighter, however, laughter can also burn out the sensibilities in you! Comedians across the globe know that people will laugh at any and everything. Comedians use language, gestures and ridicule to get people every where to laugh in the name of comedy. They will poke fun at the handicapped, crippled, blind and the lame. They will talk about the Pope, Mother Teresa, Columbine High, Charles Manson, or a fire that was set by some sick individual, all for a laugh. How insensitive, how hard and callous have we become as a society? Good hearty laughter is great and recommended, but when you can laugh at the expense of others, your finer sensibilities have been hijacked and the false you, the one that likes to dress up and be cool, will laugh at any human tragedy as long as it is expressed by the right comedian. There is nothing funny about human suffering! I do not care how you put it! Every time you laugh at a blind person, you kill your own natural sensibilities. The ability to feel for others and all creation is part of our make up as human beings. Laughter, that is not sensitive, is a killer of self-esteem and promoter of no self-control. Too much laughter is like too much food, from which you can get all kinds of physical, mental and moral problems. What is wrong with a good laugh? Nothing I guess, if you are not the butt of the insensitive tirade! I like Bill Cosby; Bill Cosby has many talents and great qualities, but one outstanding quality is his ability to make others laugh without hurting anyone. Bill Cosby has been known for decades, for good, clean and healthy comedy. You can laugh and have self-control and self-esteem also.

Laughter is a seed that can fulfill a need, can promote creeds, while spreading good deeds. Laughter is a fixer, life's elixir, if you mix her and blend her. Laughter is soothing, and smoothing. It is calming and a whole lot more.

Living Self Control

When the moment came for one of the most significant events in my life, I displayed masterful self-control. It was during a session that I had attended. As everyone else did, I volunteered to be subjected to the open and blunt criticism of all who had an opinion about me and wanted to share it. Share it they did! I had never heard nor endured such blunt, straightforward, (sometimes) vehement and honest criticism in my entire life. I had heard stronger words, but never while standing in a circle with approximately 50 or more people looking at me and seeing me for what I showed over the past 48 hours. There were no masks, no pretending, and no getting by easily. When you open up to that many people, you are bound to be have a part of your personality exposed to and for you; a part that you would normally not discuss. The purpose of this session was to "Break Through" the barriers that had long held you back from your success in life. I had more self-control than I had ever shown at any time in my life. I did not strike back! I had reason to, I had caused to, I had motive to, and I had a right to. However, striking back is not self-control; it is lack of control and poise of character. I did not realize the tremendous amount of self-control it took to endure such strong views about myself. I remember a time when I would have used adjectives, vituperative language that would shame any devil. I could remember a time when I would have torn into every one of the people in the outer circle like a "*wild wolf*" in the starving stage! I have my pride and we all have our issues; "that would have been my reasoning," however, while true, this was not about my ego and the "whisperer," this was about my self-esteem. I had self-control in me all the time, except that I had not exercised it in the the most useful manner. Most importantly, I had never recognized it. Without self-control, you are like a puppet that can be controlled by any puppeteer, who is willing, able and ready to pull your strings and watch you dance to his or her music.

The times that I did exercise self-control in my life, I came out feeling, thinking and looking good. The times when I employed this friend of mine called self-control, I not only was able to listen to others and understand their needs and wants, but, I was able to anticipate and almost knew what they were thinking! I recall being able to tell others what they were going to say. Why? I believe that, because of self-control, the ability to listen was heightened and sharpened. Any muscle that is exercised on a regular basis will get stronger and bigger. The skills of listening, smiling, thinking, and giving sincere appreciation to others, and by service to others is no different. Only through self-control can these valuable skills be heighten and honed to a point where you hear, see, feel, smell and sense things that others do not. I believe that once the self-control that I am speaking of is acquired, the individual who has such a quality is able to grant his every reasonable desire.

No matter how hard the wind blows, it cannot move a mountain!" The mountain is self-control. The wind is (in this example) anger, frustration, fear, greed, poverty, criticism, jealousy and all the other vices that can get you off course. If you have the mountain of self-control, you will command the wind and the storms of the soul to obey your every command! You will, and you must endure! Such is the power that we all possess as human beings. I am not asking you to accept or buy what I am saying; that is of little concern to me. What I am attempting to do is to show you a perspective that perhaps you have not been in touch with before; a perspective on which you may want to ponder. No amount of reading, medicine, meetings, or therapy of any kind can take the place of self-control, as it is only through this self-control that outside cures can work effectively. You have to have the desire to change, whatever it is that you desire to change. Once you have the desire it takes self-discipline and self-love to stay on course. Self-discipline is a form of self-control. Self discipline is an undeniable factor in self-control. I have learned to make self-control my dominating thought. I eat sleep and think self-control. I wake up everyday and say, *"I have great self-control and poise of character."* I also repeat this or something along these same lines several times a day! I have so thoroughly put into my subconscious mind the importance of self-control that it pops into my head without conscious effort. Self-control will guide you once you instruct your subconscious mind to accept it as your foundation, your soul's elixir! By the way, *"it is impossible to have peace of mind without self-control."* I cannot imagine any human being not desiring peace of mind. The surest way to peace of mind is this to achieve that which I keep referring to as, "self-control." I look back on my life and I can see how lack of self-control has cost me many wonderful and some great opportunities. However, I understand this important lesson, that I will never forget, "*When the student is ready, the master will appear!*" I was not ready for those opportunities and I do not feel one bit guilty about any of them. Feelings of guilt, *"especially over something that you cannot change,"* or control is a lack of self-control. I appreciate my life, and I encourage you to appreciate your life now. The fact that you are reading this book, says a lot about your willingness to change some things in your life, for the better. I see evidence of this important factor in success all around me. Look around and notice how few people have self-control and poise. In several instances you can find parents yelling at their children, spouses, or people honking horns and giving others the proverbial finger. Talk shows are popular for show-casing out-of-control mates, broken relationships and the like. Political shows have high ratings because the public demands yelling, accusing, finger pointing and slander by politicians and so called pundits. I have seen so many politicians and talk show hosts scream and yell at each other until I finally got wise and decided that I would no longer be a part of the *"lack of self-control circle."* Whether the television and news programs air conflicts for ratings or not is beside the point, which is this, *"It is promoting lack of self-control!"* I have seen and heard people in barber shops and on the public transportation argue and almost come to blows over issues raised in the media! I use to be a part of such discussion myself; hence, I am not speaking from some theory or from hearsay. I have seen employees nearly come to blows over political, racial, and other social issues. A little self-control on the part of either party would prevent these incidents and near incidents from happening. Look at the athletes who fight with fans and use foul language during interviews or in a fit of rage! Our children watch, and sadly learn from, these highly paid "out of control" men and women. Our children and adults admire them and forgive them! I am all for forgiveness many times over, but my forgiveness has nothing to do with my tuning out that garbage. One has to guard the mind from such outside suggestions that can cripple just as sure as sin planned and carried out on purpose. I turn the television and the radio off to keep out the garbage! I love my peace of mind too much to allow garbage to fester and weeds of an undesirable nature to creep in. My self-control allows me to do this and yours will too, once you make the decision. Did you notice that I said, *"Yours will too?" Yes, you do have self-control!* You may not be using it, and if not, it is weak, but, the more you exercise it, the stronger it will get, and you will be able to do whatever it takes to have great self-control.

The reason that people commit heinous crimes, lie, steal, cheat and other forms of indecencies is that they have abandoned thought control, which is self-control; anger and the wide spread hurt that is caused as a result, is lack of self-control at its worst. Envy, hatred and spite are the same, and often lead to petty crimes and sometimes murder and all kinds of malicious acts. All because the person or persons failed to exercise thought control! Self-control is strength that leads to right thoughts and positive creative actions. The person who can exercise this kind of self-control has the whole world as his or her pearl.

Your mind is the most powerful thing that exists outside of the *"Creator of All Things!"* Yet most people do not have a clue as to where to begin to go into this gold mine that we call the mind. We human beings have the ability to speak and the thing we speak will become manifest. Think a thought and what we think will come about. Ask and we will receive, as sure as the sun rises in the east and sets in the west! This book is a manifestation of all three things that I have just mentioned, namely, think, ask and speak things into existence! We all have this great ability. I will dare to call it "Power" only when we have peace of mind. Your power is your peace and, your peace is your power. This power is only potential power until it is converted into real power by stepping into your peace. This point can be easily proven in this way: when a championship team is at work, the main thing that distinguishes them from their opponent is the ability to remain calm and to think! Businesses have brainstorming sessions and master mind sessions regularly for the purpose of thinking. This thinking can only be done in a calm relaxed state. When people who lose their temper, come to their senses they often feel remorse and wish they had remained calm. People who are habitual drug abusers, alcoholics, sex-aholics, and all other kinds of holics are out of thought control, therefore they have no self-control. The form of abuse that is used by such individuals is only a getaway from the reality of being out of control with self. The human spirit is so strong and demanding that, if you do not give it the best, it will destroy you! The spirit in your will lead you to destruction and to your ultimate death because you did not make good use of the power vested in you by the Creator of All Things. The Great Spirit in you will not endure your pain, only you will. You will get assistance in every way, because your subconscious mind will make it easy for you to achieve that for which you ask. If you ask for that kind of destruction, it will see to it that you find your place in the hell of your own choosing.

The spirit has to be free and it will not tolerate your disrespect of your temple that is why it will punish you. Does not a person, who is out-of-control, deserve to be punished? Of course they do! Why? Because that is exactly what they ordered! Life and its circumstances are all made to order and you will get exactly what you order and the waitress or waiter will never confuse the order, the cook will never over cook or mix up the order. You will get exactly what you order from life whether consciously or unconsciously. Every soul you meet and come in contact with is your attraction in some way or another. This does not mean that because you come in contact with a mean spirited, criminal mind that you are a criminal mind also. It does mean that something is there for you to learn, and having learned, to move on and deposit what you have learned for your betterment and for that of others, or to achieve some worthy goal. Some people attract this kind of person, (mean spirited and/or criminal minded) because they are of the same violent unsettled mind.

In closing this section, I would like to stress the point that the laws of attraction play no favorites and will never fail! The law of compensation is exact, the law of retribution and giving and receiving are all exact! So, the next time you feel that you have not been given a fair shake, look at the things that you have spoken, acted upon and thought about. There you will find unfailing evidence of your participation in whatever life gives you. This may seem harsh and cruel, but I did not make the laws, I am subject to the same laws that you are and my pen is a witness. I too, will receive just compensation and the likes for everything that I do, think, say, and write. You can use this to your advantage for sure! You can create much good fortune if you are not too stubborn and self-doubting to do so. It just requires some time, endurance, patience, and a willingness to be totally truthful to yourself and others. Remember that, it all starts within you; it comes through you and not to you. Sufficient *self-control* will develop healthy *self-esteem* and life will be your playground at that moment

"Hot Heads" go with "cold feet."
He who loses his temper is usually a bluffer
and when "called" is a quitter

Chapter 16 Submitting Your Esteem to Others

I have seen many people work all day, all their lives, 40 hours per week to build up someone else's ego and stroke the flames of the bosses insecurities or that of their neighbors. Have you ever met someone whose very existence seems to be around pleasing a boss or the friend or some celebrity that they worship? How about people who allow others to control them and tell them how to live, what to eat and how to treat their spouses? I am not just speaking of mothers-in-law, or fathers-in-law who have their controlling issues. How about being afraid to speak out when a wrong can be corrected, but you let it pass because you were so afraid, you said nothing. You are not so much afraid of being wrong as you are of thinking about how others view your opinion. You do not feel that your opinion is educated enough to voice it. You are not a PH.D, therefore you feel you have no authority. So what do you do? Like most people do, you give your authority, your voice, your creativity to someone else, who may probably be just as afraid as you are, or have deeper issues. Yet, you wonder why things never seem to get better for you! How can they? Let us examine this, you let others control you, allow celebrity worship to run you life, by watching every award show the televisions will air in one year; you will not speak out when you ought to, and you apologize when someone asks you for a ride because your car is junky! When will you stop submitting your self-esteem to others? I have done all of the above and I have done it more than once, therefore, I am speaking from experience and not theory. Anybody with a title that sounds important, people will run too and tell their life stories, dreams, fears and sexual fantasies! Do not let them say that they are Doctor so and so; many of you will give them your account along with ATM card and pin number! Then, you take their advice and without investigation, you use it and regurgitate it as if that person were Moses bringing you a personal set of the Ten Commandments on tablets of pure gold. You feel good because you feel that you have met an important person. The sad part is that the most important person did not even get a hello from you! That most important person you will ever meet is the person who is reading this book right now, YOU! Your self-esteem is just beaten and the people and things that you worship besides "The Creator" are just a little above you in *self-esteem,* or they would not be able to stand such sucking up, bootlicking, shuffling acts, which are disguised as admiration. They are a plea for help and desperate moaning. Michael Jordan said once that he did not give autographs. He further said that he would gladly take a picture with anyone, but that he could not understand why someone would want a signature. I concur with Michael on that one. I will gladly sign this book for anyone who asks me to do so, but, I would not be in favor of just giving out signatures on blank sheets of paper or tee shirts. I would not be flattered either, because I am human and I have a need to keep my *self-esteem* in check also. There is nothing flattering about the hero worship and outright disrespect that people show because someone is a writer or in a movie. While you may be admiring them with an inordinate admiration, a zealous, frenzied, over enthusiastic admiration, many of them are barely making the grade as far as sanity is concerned. What you see in bright lights and on television is not always the real person. Celebrities commit suicide too, commit crimes, abuse spouses, and commit murder, or lie, steal and cheat too! Some do, in spite of the fact that they have enough money to feed small countries for a year! Are you sure you want to give your life to someone else? Would you not rather build your *self-esteem?* Would you not rather let the value in you shine? When many heard, *"give to receive,"* they took it to another level! You are not supposed to give your value, to anyone! In you is the key to every disease known to man, every problem that confronts us. In you are the great songs that sooth and great scientific discoveries are all in you! You not only deprive yourself when you do not value yourself, you deprive the universe of its own jewel! You have no right to act like that! Yours is the right to feel, to be and to act important and let your light shine as a paragon of success through a healthy *self-esteem* and self-confidence in your natural ability. You can not continue to submit that which is endowed on you to someone else. Should you do this, you deprive them of pieces of the puzzle that they desire. Every time that someone is admired with an inordinate admiration, some other person, has taken a shovel of dust and thrown it over their own *self-esteem,* their *self-value.* By the same token, every time someone is admired with a healthy admiration, and not glorification or deification, self-esteem is affirmed and acknowledged. Your *self-esteem* says, "Great, let's learn, grow and develop into something bigger and better!" I have been guilty of this "inordinate" admiration for a great portion of my life. I speak again, from experience and not some theory. This type of admiration always left me out of the equation. I was forgetting me and my value, my thoughts and dreams; submitting them to someone else and then would look for approval outside of me. As if, the person or persons admired did not require the same human care that we all do.

Hero Worship

Hero worship is submitting your value to another, for *self- approval.* Hero worship comes from man's innate desire to find something stronger than the self, to protect him from his fears and doubts and the malice of others. Man has created in his mind, the god of the wind, the water, the trees, the ground, the underground, the dead, the womb, the animal kingdom and the god of everything that man can create to protect himself, from himself! That is right, "from his self." Everything in nature that we look to for answers and protection is already in us. So, the seemingly natural thing to do is to seek help outside. Man has sought help through others, who are just as vulnerable as he is, but who have a bigger façade. *The façade is often fame, fortune and status.* Zeus and Thor and other gods from times gone by, are now replaced by basketball and football stars, actors, motivational speakers, scientists, painters, presidents, business men and women and the like. Man says "how ridiculous," when they read about the idol and hero worship of the past, yet, many do not see the same lived out today, on a much larger scale, and to an even more detrimental degree. How many children, teenagers and adults have you seen wearing jerseys with some athletes name on the back? How many pairs of shoes have you seen with an athletes name on them? How many times have you gone to the homes of friends and seen a wall covered with people who are well known and greatly admired? Have you ever thought about it in this way? If you are like most other people, you probably have not. In boxing, it has been said, *"it is not the punch that you see that does the most damage. It is the one that you did not see coming, which will be the one that will turn the lights out!"* Many of us do not see it coming! I love Michael Jordan, his drive and determination; his leadership and the instinct for achievement, but, I would never wear his name on my back! *What would become of me if I did that?* While this statement may not be popular with advertisers and the like, *my self-esteem* is healthy and I do not mind criticism or rejection. I can only grow from it. The issue of *self-esteem* is not new and it will not go away until it is addressed by each of us. Today, *low self-esteem* is more subtle and insidious. We become caught in a web of clutter within and without. It seems so natural to follow the crowd, that many never find its way, and heap inordinate praise on someone else's abilities and accomplishments. The cause of inner turmoil and strife can be directly linked to submitting self-esteem to others without ever even knowing it. I have given much time to discussing *low self-esteem* and very little time if any discussing, *warped or inflated self-esteem.* Yes! People can have good *self-esteem* and that same *self-esteem* can become *warped of inflated* when the individual becomes full of himself or herself. The reason for little if any discussion of these two is this, *"all of it leads to something missing in the self-esteem tank!"*

Building Self-Esteem Through Adversity

"Adversity introduces you to yourself." It shapes, molds, forms and gives you structure and style. Adversity gives you grace elegance, and refinement, and teach you empathy and love. Adversity teaches you humility, serenity, self-control and forgetful- ness of self with thoughtfulness and consideration for others. It teaches you devotion and how to harmonize your efforts. Adversity is your university of life, for without adversity, we would remain the same pile of bones, clothed with flesh, never using our power as an influence for good, and to develop peace of mind. Adversity is one of the sure ways to build a healthy self-esteem and character. You will know a man when you show him his blood, sweat and tears through adverse times and situations. Until man is exposed in adversity, you can never know the true mettle of the man.

It is at the darkest hour that we grow and achieve. Without those rainy days, storms and trials, how could we learn? How could we develop and grow? The couples who are in foreclosure, or bankruptcy or those who have creditors calling several times daily, have a jewel in front of them. The job lost, or the death of a loved one or an opportunity missed, is a golden cord that runs through the garden of paradise, waiting for you to investigate and learn from the wisdom within. You hate to be told how you really are, told about your selfishness, greed and lust for material things and for sex! You loathe being told exactly what others see in you, and few have the courage to tell us exactly as it is. You prefer *"sugar and spice,"* when a cold slap in the face of our ego is just the medicine that you need! You prefer to be told how great you are or how beautiful your voices are and how smart you are and that you are envied instead of being told how vain and selfishly motivated you are. Some of you cannot tell the truth, and have been untrue in word and deed all of your natural life, hiding in a make believe world, fantasizing on every thing from being a king to your favorite movies star, never thinking that the greatest somebody is looking in your mirror holding your toothbrush. You would rather be known for your ability to brawl and tell people off, than to be known as one who is *agreeable and pleasing.* You walk around hurting, in pain and agony, knowing full well that the amount of money you earn is making you miserable, be it small or a considerably large amount. The IRS calls and sends those letters that you dread and you panic and run for cover, never thinking, *"There is a gold cord in this situation that I am to learn and develop from."* You seemingly fail at everything that you have ever tried to accomplish, but the reality is, you gave up on everything because you are suffering and you feel that old age is getting the better of you. You fear everything from being overweight, to people knowing that you have false teeth! You fear death, destruction and embarrassment of all kinds. Do you not understand that *"what you fear is what you will attract?"*

You blame the government, the city and the media for your problems and lack of achievement. You blame your spouses and friends and everything and everybody for your lack of ambition and the hurts and pain that you suffer. You often dream of and speak of the thing that you desire, but, you show no willingness to learn from the *adversity*, which carries with it the seed of the thing that you seek. You run from problems (*which are opportunities)* to acquire the things that you pray for, yet you have no courage to go through the fire to get them. Yes! Go through the fire! Fire burns and purifies as well as destroys. We are talking about the purifying fires of the soul. *Adversity* teaches a man how to go though the fire and burn off all the lies, facades and phony show that we display. The fires are in our lives to melt away the mask; the pretentiousness, and to live life abundantly. The only thing that you can grow from is your crisis, except that you learn from the experience of others and apply it. The best and surest way to learn is through every life experience that comes your way, be they favorable or not. Oh, some of you are in a fire now. The fire that you are in is not the one that burns off the excess and the hindrances to your character and personality; fires that burn in you are the ones that burn you up, and out! That is the fire of so called *"Hell!" I am not finished yet!*

You salesman! You who are in the greatest most rewarding profession in the world, when are you going to stop lying to people and making up stories to make a sale? We see you! We see the façade and the duplicity in you. We see your crime, your sin, your smooth, glib rhetorical bunk. When are you going to develop the kind of character that will attract business to you? You cannot fake sincerity and honesty; you cannot fake being real; either you are or you are not. You want to brag about being number one this month, yet you know that you did some things that you are ashamed to mention in public to secure your status. Yes! This is adversity that you are going through while reading this. If you have the courage, keep reading and go through some more. Life is not going to be as easy to you as I am. I love you and I can understand you. However, life's purpose is neither to understand you, nor to empathize with you; life will only (*can only)* give you what you put out, *what you attract.* That is the hard, cold, and often harsh reality. I am not afraid to tell you that you have been unjust to yourself and everyone you love, or are supposed to love. Maybe you have become callous and insensitive, one who will laugh at any joke about anybody, whether they are crippled or blind. I love you; I am not trying to hurt you or injure you in any way; my mission is to awaken you so that you can witness the great inner peace that I have come to learn by being true to myself. I love you; I am your brother in this thing called "life." I feel it is my duty to tell you about the *self* that you think is your real self, so that I can get you to see that *true self* that you have imprisoned for all of your life. I love you. I love you enough to tell you how ugly you look when you fly off the handle in a fit of rage and say things that would shame one thousand devils. I love you enough to tell you that such behavior only reveals your cowardice and lack of moral courage. I love you enough to tell those *who use the church and the pulpit,* for selfish, monetary gain and a puffed up sense of self, to quit manipulating those souls who are just a little weaker than you. I am not going to hold back, because that is your problem now. I have seen many people who have been attracted to a career in preaching, and who claim that they have been called by God, and that they must collect tithe every Sunday. I definitely admire those who are true and sincere and, I encourage them to continue in their good work. I recommend *tithing* to all, but, I have nothing but rebuke and more rebuke for those who mislead in the name of God and Christ! With regard to the claim that they have been called by God, I often wonder about which god they are really talking, since they twist and turn scripture to read as they wish, to represent their own desires and wishes, while failing to admit one thing: *"Their beliefs result from what they have been told."* Further, they have done very little soul searching for the hidden jewels in the Holy Bible! I love you enough to warn you not to fall within this group, lest you become as a parrot with a book in one hand and a collection plate in the other, and give a bad name to the great field of bringing spiritual enlightenment to the world. The church and places of worship have done much good in societies around the world, however, much of the work has been disastrous and murderous of a mental, and spiritual nature. Not to mention the blood that has been spilled in the name of religion. I am not talking about any particular religious belief, for I can find sincerity and insincerity on all sides. Do not get puffed up and think that I am not talking about you; Cast your ego off today, because we will not tolerate it here!

Why keep deceiving yourself? You are not deceiving us, those who know better! When are you going to stop playing the game of destruction and grief, and have peace and true relief? When are you going to live life on natural terms and drop the cow manure? When are you going to stand up like a natural human being and *"Be"* the great and wonderful creature that you are made to be? I love you and I always will. You writers! When are you going to stop writing just to get a buck or a number one best seller? When will the desire to service your dear reader be your chief aim in life? When will you learn to give more and do more than you are paid to do? How can you do this if all of your material is some fluff fluff, thank you ma'am, and half-hearted flower that you don't have a real clue about? When are you going to awaken your *self-esteem* and realize that the greatest thing that you could write, is that which comes from your own soul? It will be a number one best seller, because no one else can have your valuable experience. Some of you deprive the world of the jewels that are inside of you, by showing off with your "Big Name" endorsers, and talk about what you have experienced when you know that much of it is just filler to get published, and to have others say, "He or she is somebody." You are already somebody, you are the best somebody and nobody could ever rival your greatness! When are you going to see this and come real and legitimate? When your motives are not right, *"you are being a nobody that could be somebody, if only you would accept yourself as somebody."* Writers! Let us bow our heads in prayer and meditation and pray that the *Creator* grant us humility, peace of mind and pure intent in the game of life.

I love entertainers and performers in concert and in recordings; I have great respect and love for those who bring the universal language of music to the world. I have deep admiration for those whose lyrics inspire, promote and devote love to many around the world. I love the words of those artists that truly use their craft to better the lives of others. I love the dance that speaks volumes for the human soul and capacity for true creativity. However, I have no time for the trash! Keep the garbage and the filth! I promise you that, "if you put the garbage in your trunk and go into the studio and perform from the greatness within you, no one, will even inquire about the filth." I will not even bother to go into the sad and degrading state of politics these days; the majority of the politicians ought to be ashamed, and they know it! The better of the bunch are a small minority to whom we should show our appreciation, and sincere gratitude.

This has been *controversial and challenging* for some of you who are reading this and I applaud you! I applaud you if you got upset but kept on reading. I applaud you if you looked into your soul and saw some things that you desire to improve on. I applaud you for being up front with yourself. You have demonstrated great self-control by continuing to read on, especially if some of what you have just read may have hit home. I respect you and encourage you to have a deeper respect for yourself. This has been a breakthrough for many of you; one that could last you for the rest of your life. Build on what you have discovered about *you and adversity, and* learn to learn from every situation possible. All these things that happen in our lives are brick and wood and all the tools to build healthy *self-esteem. I have spoken and written from the soul in this chapter, as I have in every chapter in this book. I have not pointed an accusing finger at you without first pointing several at me. I love you and only desire the best for you.*

Remember that, *"Adversity is like a golden cord running through the garden of paradise."* Adversity is often, and more often than not, disguised brilliantly! The key is to remove your mask, and drop all the facades and discover the *golden cord.* One man who was in his mid sixties and was receiving a social security check for a little more than one hundred dollars a month decided to be rich and famous. Adversity did not defeat him; his name is "Colonel Harland Sanders!" Kentucky Fried Chicken is a household name today and around the world!

"Adversity causes some men to break; others to break records." ***William A. Ward***

Chapter 17 Peace Is an Imperative

Peace means: *"To be healthy, whole, successful, safe and sound, complete, gentle, and incontrovertible, and to deliver and to receive!* Peace means: *"To touch to graze, and to take possession."* Peace means: *"to surrender, and abandon." Abandon what? It means to abandon your self-sabotage and silence the chatter box. It means to get the chatter to conform to, and succumb to your command, and that is where you will find and have peace of mind!* Peace means, *"to be certain, to be established and clearly proven, to be free!" Freedom is the goal of the student, and peace is the means to the freedom. Peace means to process and progress smoothly.*

Doesn't this definition of peace give you a clearer and broader view of the word? Is it not wonderful to know that peace has so many facets, and is not just related to someone who says little and nods wisely, as if the wisdom of the world resides only in him? What can a healthy and clear definition of the word "peace" do for you? After this portion of the "Reclining Master," I believe that one cannot remain the same, knowing that the key to all that you have aspired to become is directly correlated to your understanding of and embracing eternal "peace" as a way of life, and not just as an academic exercise to which you pay lip service, or as a convenient word.

To live and exist with assurance of the best that life can offer, "Peace" must be an imperative. Peace means "deliverance" and security. I know that this meaning may be foreign to some of you, but think about it. Peace is the only thing that can relieve you of the pain and suffering of yesterday, worries about things that may happen tomorrow, and all kinds of challenging circumstances. Peace is the great deliverer, and too few people view it this way. The way of peace is the way to freedom. Peace cannot be an option or a "maybe," because if it is, your mind will be like a sponge that takes in everything whether desirable or undesirable. Be careful of what you allow to enter into your mind! The seed that you allow to take root today will manifest in the circumstances of tomorrow! Whatever you plant, be sure that it is with peace of mind. The reason for so much turmoil and stress in people is that they lack peace of mind. There can never be a situation where there is never any chaos; there would be no need for peace if chaos did not exist. Whatever you have in your mind, you will attract that same thing to you in the outer world. It is like wanting ice cream, but getting fire instead! The only way to get fire instead of ice cream is to go to the wrong place, and order the wrong thing, by not making what you desire clear and precise. When you have stress, turmoil and unrest in your life, you can expect a full plate of the same. I call it, *"The Law of the Mirror!"* The law of attraction is what you may be familiar with; in any case, it is the same. So one should be careful to select one's thoughts and be on guard for any outside thoughts or influences that can upset the balance of the good and peace of mind that you aspire to have. The plot of ground on which the farmer plants his crops, is an outer replica of how the mind operates. The mind can only return to you what you plant in it, nothing more, and nothing less.

Peace as the "Receiver"

When you have attained peace, you will receive, because to be peaceful is to be receptive, and like will always attract like. When you give peace, you will receive some great and wonderful things in return. Peace opens the way for more receiving and giving. When you have peace, you will want to share it and give it to others; abundance is attracted to peace and tranquility. The more tranquil and peaceful we become the greater our success and growth. This can be further explained by nature and the way things naturally flow. Everything in nature has a flow and a peace. There is not chaos but order in everything in the universe, so everything runs in course in perfect timing except *ego driven* man! Of all things animate or inanimate, man is the only one that will, by choice, go against the peace and create chaos. When we do, we block the smooth progress toward the attainment of our full potential. Peace releases your own creative power and acumen. Peace is what makes your decisions sound and right. Only a mind that is not at peace waver, wander to and fro, fearing that the wrong decision has been made. Indecision, which is procrastination, is a result of having a "lack of peace of mind." Once this is understood and action is taken to acquire that inner peace, the external conditions and circumstances must correspond.

Three Stages to Peace of Mind

The first stage in the process is *"command or direct."* You can direct and command the mind to do your bidding at every level and at every stage. You are lord and master of your mind and you have power to direct it to do as you wish. This is great in that, you can deliberately plan, determine and bring about what you deeply desire, however you cannot force or make someone else's reality correspond to yours. Your power is yours, and so it is with everyone else. Your mind cannot disobey you! It can only follow what you put in it, or tell it with complete submission. It will not talk back or disobey the command or even question it; it will only be your loyal and trusted servant. You have total influence on your mind; it takes whatever instructions it receives as "an imperative." It will not and cannot distinguish between right and wrong. Once instructed, it will do your bidding automatically, with time and constancy. Once the mind has been instructed and thoroughly conditioned to follow a certain pattern, or to plant certain thoughts, it will develop that characteristic and you will then be a person of self-control and poise, but not until the three stages are achieved.

The second stage is the stage of rapprochement and self-examination. This is the stage where you are on guard and conscious of thoughts of an unclean nature and things that are counter to your peace of mind. This is the stage where self-control is developed and honed to the point where none can enter into your mind and deposit their issues and life problems and mental diseases. This is where you are vigilant and you censure *(self)* thoughts of destructive or seductive nature. This is when you take your time and learn patience by watching the workings and the process of thoughts that attempt to invade your castle. At this point in consciousness, you will find yourself reprehending certain thoughts for trying to get into the soil of your mind. I have referred to this source as the *"Whisperer,"* throughout this book. This whisperer must be rebuked and reprehended often until it is thoroughly and dominantly subdued! It takes will, desire, and effort. However, the main thing is that you are now aware of it, and you realize that it is all in your control, or power to do as you please. Reading this has opened you up to yourself! You can never blame anyone but the person in the mirror, as you can only look to yourself or inside yourself to find out what goes on.

The third and final stage is the stage of calm, tranquility and serenity of mind. After enough time and desire to acquire peace of mind, at this stage you have it; ease, assurance, composure and trust. You have confidence and self-control, and no one can get you out of your peace, and if they do, you will get back in a flash! At this point, the mind will be on automatic pilot. When outside suggestions or self-suggestions that do not harmonize with the beautiful garden that you have planted attempt to come in, they will be rejected and pursued by a flaming guard! This guard is a protector grown out of the thoughts that you created to arrive at this state of mind. You power is in your peace! You cannot think, grow and master life without this peace of mind. It is more valuable than gold. People seek riches, fortunes, and sexual gratification for the way those things will make them feel. The money, the power, and/or sexual gratification are symbols of a deeper craving, and that is to feel important, to feel outrageous joy, well-being, self love and inner peace. Many soon learn that (material) things alone, do not bring peace of mind, and as a result, cannot bring contentment. At this third stage of the mind, you are in the *House of the Master* of the ages! All great minds have arrived at this point and this is what makes the truly great ones great! Napoleon Hill wrote; *"Edison was far and away the calmest man I have every known. He had no frustration. He had no fears. He had no regrets about anything or anyone. He had no grandiose ideas of his own importance, but he did have humility of the heart, which made him truly great."* If you are true to yourself, and accept the ideas put down in this section on peace of mind with the desire and determination to change your life, and to empower others to do the same, *"You will gain mastery!"* We have a "Mind" free and clear; flowing from the great own exalted image of the ALL, according to the language of scripture. I doubt that we would have been endowed with the most powerful machine in all creation without the ability and the power to put it to work to do our most rewarding bidding. We can be down trodden and slothful, or we can rise to the heights of wonderful life achievement; both are our choice to make. Not to use our mind and direct it towards peace and attainment is sin!

Poise, Poise, Poise

Poise is the goal! Poise is the key to having and maintaining a balanced state of mind; keeping your emotions in line with your peace. When something happens that cause you to be overjoyed or wildly enthusiastic and you scream and holler, "that is not poise." When something happens that saddens you or cause you grief and you are on the floor screaming and talking about how unfair life is, "you are out of balance;" that is not poise. The goal is poise, the calm and the middle emotional state. What do I mean by, *"middle emotional state?"* The middle emotional state is where you can take what happens in life and *keep your highs low and your lows high*. This is a state of serenity and calm; this is having control and self-confidence in you. At this stage in your development, you are trusting your feelings and relying on your power to handle any situation. Being poised is being courageous; and courage is an inside job. When you have the courage to exercise poise, your mind can process the information and the resultant situation for what it is really worth, and more often than not, the things that make us overly enthusiastic or down in the dumps are not as bad as we make them out to be. I have had many times in my life when I would get nervous and upset over small things, but I learned to stay calm and think. When I started to calm down or stay cool and think, I always came up with an answer to my situation. I recall a string of instances where I did not have money to attend 3 different events. Each time that this happened, I sat down early in the morning when the birds were sleep. There with a sheet of paper in hand, I sat thinking, and as thoughts came to me I would write them down. These thoughts took shape and formed ideas, which I wrote, and with the ideas I received, came names and a plan of action! Each time, I followed the plan of action and each time I solved the problem. Each name I called, every professional or person, had a lesson of value that I was seeking, on some level. Every one of them was helpful to some part of my life in that moment. These three instances were only separated by two months each. The principles I am talking about are not theory, "they are practical and have been proven time and time again!" They have been proven by me, in my life; why not you, and in your life now, today? Poise! The goal of the reader, the student and the teacher is poise! Poise allowed me to think and the right person, place and thing came to mind. Nervousness, chaos, worry, grief, anxiety and anger, all block the thought process; thoughts can have no free expression when there is not a flow of peace, therefore poise. Poised, the mind is served; the mind is served with space, air and a clean canvass to operate from and to draw the diagram for solving the situation or the problem. Without this space, air and a clean or clear canvass, the mind is cluttered, stuffed up and clouded. Which would you prefer? The answer seems obvious. However, I am not so convinced that everyone wants to flow and have poise. Some people have become so accustomed to chaos and clutter in the mind, that anything that threatens to disturb that environment is viewed as an enemy, to be fought at every appearance. There have been times when people that I would meet or have known for some years would seem to avoid me, because I am not a chaos attic or a clutter monster. How do I know this? I know this by their conversation and their demeanor. Likewise, they also know by my demeanor and poise that I will not tolerate nor make allowances for drama in my life. I am constantly studying and observing my motives, "whether or not they are of fear or faith, daily." I am a seeker of peace and right thought, with great self-control, knowing that I can only attract to my reality that which I truly am. One important point I would like to express is this, "We are all connected to learn from each other." Whether someone is a chaos attic or a drama major, or an angry tyrant, there is a valuable lesson to be learned. While others saw a lifeless stone, *Picasso saw an angel in that boulder! Although he was deaf, Beethoven heard symphonies of nature, and recorded them, while others heard the rushing streams and the chirps of birds and nothing more!* Poise is the goal, poise is the goal, and again, poise is the goal of the student of the game! Poised, one can see the possibilities and act accordingly, thus claim the prize of your achievement and then move to the next exciting adventure.

"Only the Wise Man,
Only He Whose Thoughts Are Controlled
And Purified Makes The Winds and The
Storms Of The Soul Obey Him"

Chapter 18 The All Important Attitude

The world can only give you what you put out. There is no simpler way that I can put it. Your attitude is a direct reflection of what you are and, what you will receive. Show me a person with a great attitude toward life, and I will show you a person whose life is great. Show me a person whose attitude is poor, and I will show you a person whose life is poor. It does not matter how much money one earns or how many worldly possessions one may have acquired, the measure of success is much broader, with peace of mind taking precedence over all things. If you have an expectant attitude and an attitude of thankfulness for being a part of life, then you are on the road to success in a higher sense of the word. The generic sense of success is often money and all the material possessions that one can amass in a lifetime. But, that is the attitude of success that makes *"things and money"* the master. When the attitude of success is peace of mind, *"you"* become the master, and the money and the things become the *servant!* Is that not a novel idea? Nothing beats a cheerful, happy attitude; a calm and pleasing countenance that says, "I appreciate you and I am interested in your wants and desires." Nothing will beat an attitude that causes you to smile with the brightness of the morning sun at its brightest! You never know whose world you are going to light up; sometimes, it is a smile or a simple "how are you," that can start another on the road to a successful day. Here is another thought, *"your smile and warm appreciation shown for others, will light you up, and carry you to many more happy and successful days!"* Who ever said *"happiness is an inside job,"* certainly knew something about human nature. If you give love and show happiness, and appreciation for life, life will give it back to you. Life will give you more than you give! You cannot out give life! It is called the law or increasing returns. There is no such thing as *"something for nothing."* However, here is a novel idea to some of you; *"You cannot have something without anything!"* You must give something, where there is nothing to get something. That is a twister to think about. The more you ponder it, the more sense it will make and the more use you can make of the law of increasing return. Our attitudes are contagious and those closest to us can feel and sense the attitude that we harbor deeply. It is not something that can be faked or done half-heartedly. When our attitudes are genuine, (from *the heart* of our being) others will know it, and will respond to us in kind. As you sow, so shall you reap! That statement is the essence of who and what we are as human beings. That statement is the other half of why we were created. We were created to have wonderful attitudes by rendering service to the *Creator* of all things first; and secondly, we were created to give, sow, and receive, reap, and to manifest the glory of the Creator; by bringing plenty out of little, whether material or otherwise, and to bring justice and truth. We can make manifest his glory in our lives.

Commitment

One of the biggest obstacles in the way of "would be achievers" is indecisiveness. The ability to respond, make decisions and take action is a sign of emotional, rational, and overall inner maturity. By *mature* I mean, *"A mind that is capable of making decisions and taking action without guilt or hesitancy."* Hesitancy and guilty feelings about making decisions and taking action are born of fear and doubt; which is not real. This fear and doubt, which is manifested as indecisiveness and doubt, can often be traced to childhood experiences. The thought of taking very little or no risk has been implanted in a child's mind if he is often told, "*Keep your money, you might loose it, or I know a friend that lost money in one of those business ventures.*" *Words are the tools of thought;* the more we understand words, the more we will come to understand our inner dialogue and ourselves. Without this *Maturity which is Commitment* to make decisions and take action in relation to our dreams, goals and desires, we are no better than puppets; we stagnate and lack the skills necessary to develop into bigger, stronger, and more creative minds. *Commitment* instills in us the will to stay the course! Until you have this valuable tool, you are simply wandering aimlessly. No amount of pretense and no façade can conceal this "*lack of commitment.*" That is like trying to put a flaming inferno under a stack of paper that is soaked with gasoline. It won't work! The moment you open your mouth, you proclaim to the world your commitment or not. The majority may not notice or even care, but, there are some (and not a few) who can see; these people will recognize you the moment you open your mouth! Why do you think that prospective employer ask, "Are you looking for a career?" The canned answer is yes; merely to get the job. However, trained interviewers can determine your level of commitment by reading your body signals and eye movement. If you have ever wondered why you did not get a job, this may have been why. It is not always the case; however, if you show no ability to commit, you probably will not get hired. Employers would ask me, "*Why do you jump around so much?*" They were saying, *"You are not a committed person."* I understood it and I smiled every time, knowing that I had a career that I wanted to develop; I was not willing to spend 25 years developing someone else's dreams. I did not lack commitment; *I lacked the desire to burn my desire and talents on someone else's dreams and visions.* There is a distinct difference to say the least.

Thoughts and Commitment

Your self-value, your self-approval and your self-confidence make it easy for you to commit. Commitment alone is not the core or the matter. The core issue is *self-value,* but behind it all is the power of your thoughts! Once you have enough value or belief in your own self-worth, commitment becomes first nature. The fears and doubts and lack of maturity with our inner self are rooted in a *low or warped self-value.* I believe that, "*low self-value"* is the cause in most cases. Does this mean that a person who commits always has healthy *self-value?* Not At All! It all depends on what the individual commits to and for what reason. For instance, a person may commit to working 40 hours a week for 40 years; that is a commitment and one that should be applauded, especially if the person is happy. But, I have known many people who have committed in this same way; they walk with their heads to the ground and, rarely have I met one that was truly happy. We are speaking of 95% of people in America and possibly in the entire world. I hear people repeating phrases like, "*Commitment to excellence and striving to be the best.*" Yet most do not have a clue as to where it all begins. The *commitment and the striving* must be inward to manifest in outward circumstances. That is where so many people miss the mark. How you view it is how you do it! Thoughts will guide you to look outward just as you have instructed it too! You will never find what you seek if you are looking in all the wrong places. When I came to understand this, my life took on miraculous meaning. I found true happiness through commitment and striving for my dreams and heart's desires. My mother told us years ago, when we lived in a 2 bedroom, 1 bathroom apartment in Chicago, *"Thoughts are Things."* I have never forgotten those words and they have proved to be true all the days of my life. Once you are committed and strive for your hearts desires, your thoughts will fuel your advancement towards your goals. That is why positive thinking is so vital to your survival; when times get tough, (as they sometimes will) your positive thoughts will give you the energy needed to continue on. Negative thoughts drain your energy and are a haven for fears and doubts.

Take it easy, and let it flow

We are most powerful when we learn to relax and let things flow through us. This was particularly difficult for me to grasp, as I was always one who wanted to make things happen. It is *"Being"* that most people do not understand, therefore they suffer what is not necessary to suffer and vibrate and attract things to their reality that are counter to there true desire. One of the reasons that people do not allow their lives to flow is because of limiting, self-denying beliefs.

To download a copy of my ebook, "*Release and Advance Confidently,"* go to www.esteemnow.com

Chapter 19 Character

Emerson said:

"Human character does evermore publish itself. It will not be concealed...it rushes into light...I heard an experienced counselor say that he never feared the effect upon a jury of a lawyer who does not believe in his heart that his client ought to have a verdict. If he does not believe it, his unbelief will appear to the jury... and will become their disbelief.... that which we do not believe we cannot adequately say, though we may repeat the words ever so often...

A man passes for what he is worth. What he is, engraves itself on his face, on his form, on his fortunes, in letters of light which all men may read but himself...Every violation of truth is not only a sort of suicide in the liar, but is a stab at the health of human society....Trust men and they will make it their business to trust you; treat them greatly and they will show themselves great."

Man may think that his thoughts, his feelings and even his motive can be kept secret, and they can be. But only to those who are as blind and naïve as they are! The words we speak, the thoughts we think, the deeds we perform, and the smiles on our faces along with our handshake, and voice tones and variations, speak volumes about our character. *Character is what we are;* no one can make character, for it is what we have become. Every breath we take tells the world who or what we are, the sum total of our words and expressions revealed thus to the universe. You can no more hide your character than you can put an elephant under the hood of a Volkswagen! Character is something that speaks when you sleep, eat, disagree, laugh, play, work, make love, dance and/or sing. Character is something that animal's sense in man. Character tells all with whom you come in contact that you are trust worthy or un-trustworthy. Character tells prospective clients in their gut if they wish to do business with you or not. I have been in situations where I sold home improvement products to clients who had spoken to other salesmen who sell the same products for fewer dollars. Yet, I would get the sale! Why? They said, "We like you and feel that you are an honest man." Yes, they did say, "We like you." I have been on the other end of the stick also, when someone did not purchase from me for the opposite reason, although they did not say it, "I felt it." In both instances my character was a determining factor in the sale. Character is the misunderstood ingredient in life's journey to happiness. How can one be happy without sound and good character to buttress his every thought, act and deed? Every smile, genuine or pretentious, shows and admits to character. Every eyebrow raised and every sneeze and cough reveals character. Every time we eat, go to the restroom, drive or park our cars, we reveal character. Every song written and every walk taken reveals character. Every act of intimacy and every act of envy and/or jealousy reveals our character and introduces us to ourselves. Every sickness, loss of a loved one or joke laughed at, reveals character. Every thrill that one gets from watching a horror movie, a concert or a prizefight reveals character! Character is who we are! We need more mirrors in our homes and dwellings and fewer forms of entertainment only to right ourselves! Character draws to Itself that which is in harmony with itself, repels that which is not in harmony with it, and makes calm the storms and the tempest of the soul. It does each in season and in perfect timing. It is true that, one only needs to right him self, in order to right the things in the world outside of himself. It amazes me how people will go to great lengths to get a job or to obtain a passing grade for a college degree, yet, on the other hand, the same people will not spend or devote one month to the development of character. I opine that the reason for this lies in a lack of respect for self and our intrinsic value. Too many people overvalue what they are not, and under value what they are! What you are is what the world is all about! Until you take sufficient time and give proper attention to your character development, you will never know peace of mind. You must *"know yourself"* before you can acquire peace of mind; character is the doorway to such peace and harmony of self. If you would be great, be great! If you would be grand and marvelous, be grand and marvelous! If you would be magnificent, calm and poised, be magnificent, calm and poised! If you would be loved and revered, love and revere yourself, and you will be love and revered! If you would be a scholar, an inventor, a great writer or musician, then be a scholar, an inventor, a great writer or musician. BE and it is! Let it BE written, so let it BE done on earth as it is in heaven! The divine plan for your life is already set for you but you must have the courage to find it and act upon it. Yes, it is already written and done and all you have to do is *till the soil;* no one has the key accept you. While many of you are engaged in glorified admiration of someone else, you are neglecting your wondrous abilities. No matter how well defined and poised the character of another may be, yours is and always will be the most important to the world. I have come to this conclusion by my own thinking, *"fear is the great tyrant of character."* People fear what they are and dread the idea that they are more, therefore can do more and simply BE, without explanation or contemplation; BEING without anyone's approval, requires art and courage. Being like a child! Ah! That is a novel idea. A great man, some two thousand years ago spoke about it in this manner according to this source, *"I assure you, unless you turn from your sins (fear and doubt) and become as little children, you will never get into the kingdom of heaven."* Being like a child is in no way suggesting that you not take life seriously, it is suggesting that we take ourselves like angels and be light in our souls. Children are happy, cheerful and full of love. Children act, do and feel from the heart and they forgive and let things flow. Children are not afraid to be *who they really are.* Children do not try to be, they simply "BE." Children have peace, and peace is where your power is; peace is where all things are shaped and formed for your benefit and for the benefit of others. In your peace you create your heaven, and the lack of it creates your hell. Peace is the last lesson of culture, refinement, and poise and of the finished character! No character is ever finished nor cultivated without the poise that only peace within can bring. When you have peace, you have posture, which is not something you try to have. Posture is something that comes with peace and calmness of mind and heart. The strength of your character will be in direct proportion to the extent of your peace. Character is best defined as "*Peace in Action.*" Some may contend that "*bad character*" is not peace in action, and I agree! I agree only in some aspect of understanding the point. However, I believe the term, "*bad Character,*" to be an oxymoron. That, to me, is like saying, *"jumbo shrimp."* One of the greatest challenges of human beings is to build strong, solid and reliable character. Your character tells the world what you really are, not what you want the world to think of you. You can no more hide character than you can hide an elephant behind a single rose. *We See Who You Really Are, No Matter What You Think or Choose To Believe!* One of the greatest gifts that the Creator of all things gave us is, "the ability to change." The remarkable thing is that we can choose to build our character to our own liking, by the words we internalize and speak, the thoughts we think and the peace we come to have by learning to stand still. I am thoroughly convinced that we may become whatever we like, whatever we dream of and whatever we desire in our hearts. The world is full of ideas and well meaning people who will tell you what to think and how to be, but, the truth is this, "All systems, manners, attitudes, methods, and ways and means work!" They all work, whether they are of a mean and harsh spirit, or a calm and peaceful spirit. Mean hearted tyrants can achieve material success just as individuals who adhere to golden rules. Soft-spoken sales people can go as far as direct, powerful speaking sales people. Fast-talking and moving individuals who are decisive can achieve what seemingly more patient people can achieve. The point is this, people are always talking about how to be and how not to be, but the hard facts are, you can go anyway you like and achieve the same material worth." The distinct difference is, *"Peace of Mind and Happiness!"* To be truly happy and to have peace of mind requires a different attitude and there are no exceptions to this rule. If you would like to build your character so that you may enjoy these in abundance, then the *inner self* becomes the main object of your quest to succeed; all other quests and desires will take on a different meaning. *Peace and Happiness* becomes the objective and the material accomplishments are the resulting circumstances of what is within. You can have the material things without peace and happiness or you can have peace and happiness without the material things However, you can have both but it's all up to you. I will not say which is right, the best or the most fulfilling way; you must choose that for your self. I have chosen how I wish to proceed with my life and you must do the same for yours. If you do not make a conscious choice and decision, someone else will make one for you, which is the way most people live. *You are not like most people, because if you were, you would not be reading this book.* Now, I understand human tendency to deny, dismiss and take lightly what has been said about character and the importance of it. However, once you have read this, it will stay with you and you will remind yourself time and time again that, you are responsible for what you attract by being what you are in character. Read that last sentence again and again, until you memorize it! It will be well worth it to your career.

Is it not true that knowing and accepting this point on character makes you a person of a *"responsible character?"* Is not life about being responsible and taking charge of your life by molding and developing your character to be the person you desire to be; to have the things and people in your life that you deserve? Do you not want the kind of character that others long for, look for, and deeply desire to be around? Do you not deserve the best for yourself and your loved ones? Do you not desire to be an example of sound, good character for others? If the answers are "Yes" to these questions, then I know that you will listen to the tapes, read the books, attend the seminars, and do whatever is necessary to develop the character and poise that will fulfill the life of your desires. There is no doubt in my mind that everyone reading this would love to have, maintain and even build on great character. The question is, *"Are you willing to do whatever it takes, to get what you want?"* This may not be the proper question here, but, "*Are you willing to do, in order to have?"* For many of you, the jury is still out. However, I will predict the verdict for you. The verdict is this, *"You will, you must and you definitely take the right actions to build a good solid character."* Remember that, *"Reputation is what others give you; Character is what you build; the sum total of what you think habitually."*

Character, Pressure and Endurance

The more and the greater the pressure, the stronger the character will become if pressure is endured. The challenges that come with millionaire or billionaire status is to strengthen the character. People with lots of money are not people without pressures and life's challenges; they are often people who understand that the game is about endurance, overcoming, giving and receiving. With each level, be it physical, financial or spiritual, *"There Is a New Devil or Reality!"* The big goals bring big challenges, while the little goals bring little challenges. The reward is in the process and in the harvest. The reaping is the reward no matter what field you are in, the rules never change. The rewards without fail go to those who endure! Everything is about enduring trials and tribulation, and if you can withstand the pressure calmly, you can receive an abundance of the goods that you seek. Endurance is one of the marvelous *"Hall Marks"* of character, in that it announces to the world, to the universe, what the man that endures or does not endure is made of. There is an old saying that states, "Pressure will burst a pipe!" There is an old Russian proverb that says, "The hammer shatters glass, but it forges steel!" Those that burst are those that gave in to life's trials and pressures, and those who endure are those who were forged out of the same pressures. Great things come to those who wisely endure!

Loud Music (Noise Pollution)

In today's fast moving world it is often that you can drive down the streets and hear music booming and see cars shaking from the vibration of the stereo sound and power. It is almost like a concert on wheels these days, and is called *"noise pollution,"* by many cities and counties throughout the United States. To some it can be costly because they are required to pay fines for noise pollution, which is exactly what it is. The pollution occurs in more subtle and insidious ways than most would suspect. I understand why the music is loud and why people feel a need to always have the television on in the home. For example, many times I hear the television on in my home when no one is watching it. It is a scary to think that you allow into your mind, thoughts that you have no idea of where they are coming from. In most broadcasts, there is always a message, usually one is open and one is sometimes hidden. People are afraid to face who they really are. When I see people riding in their cars with windows up or down and the music just blasting away, without consideration for others on the road, I understand that those individuals are often hiding from the self. When I see people come home and flop on the sofa and flip through the channels to see what is on, I cannot help but wonder, "Does this person know or have the slightest notion that they are robots and not free thinkers?" These are people who drown out reality by turning up the music, or turning the television on. But, there is something even subtler than this: they are drowning out the inner voice that speaks so loudly they do not want to hear nor understand it. People are afraid of who they really are; loud music and constant television viewing is an escape from what is. What is most ironic is, "The reality of who they are is their greatest strength, because that is where *"perfect self-expression" can* be found. Our greatness resides in our true self. While music has wonderful qualities and comforting agents for the mind, body and spirit, the loud and booming constant sound of music and television actually drowns out your peace of mind. There is no real enjoyment in the music that is so loud that you cannot hear your own voice when you speak. What you often have is a purely emotional experience; the same is true with loud television. The words Tel and Vision say it all! Your vision is being told, whether you like it or not and your mind is being fed some other program which may be totally out of line with what you desire deep down in your inner self. And, it usually is out of line with your true self. The experience of loud music and constant television viewing leaves you vulnerable in the most dangerous way. There is an inner voice in all of us, and sometimes this is referred to as *intuition, a hunch, a gut feeling or psyche*. Whatever you choose to call it, know this, "*It is there and it is real!*" This inner voice or calling is what gives life that deeper meaning, direction and assurance, and without it life is chaotic and full of turmoil. Why? Because you have value beyond measure and no mind, thought or genius is as important as yours. No sage, wise man or woman, no writer, speaker or king can produce the genius that is latent in you. The more you drown the sound of the inner voice in you and never take the time to think, meditate and pray, the more callous you become to this power source that is rarely understood, but all great men and women attest to its presence and contribution to their success.

The loud music is "coating" the façade, or the mask that people wear. The loud boomers are saying, *"I am not comfortable with who and what I am, so I'll just pretend to be so in love with this music that no one will notice the real me."* Many of us notice and we see you not as you wish to be seen, but as you are! Music is great and soothing, however, not as a way to escape our self-expression. To be overly enthused about someone else's talent is inherently dangerous to the creativity of the over enthusiastic admirer. For years I used loud music as a means of escape and as a retreat from the known. The known was this, *"I was not living to my full potential, and I feared success and who I really was."* The music would allow me to live in a fantasy world, while believing deeply that I was of little value and the people that I listened to were important, and that I had to be like them to be as important. This was and still is a sort of ghetto culture. I am not speaking of any one culture or race of people; instead, I am talking about *"low self-esteem ghetto style."* Loud music is a seemingly harmless, but very hypnotizing means of escape. Look at the words "*Harm –less."* The word references *harm,* but it is saying, "You will experience" *less* harm. That is very much like saying, "I am going to shoot you, but instead of using a 38 caliber bullet, I'll use a 22 caliber bullet and cause you less harm! I am sure you would not object to that; or would you?

Just by reading the first chapter of this book, anyone who reads *"The Reclining Master,"* will know that *Earth, Wind & Fire* played a significant role in my life and the positive road that I have chosen; there can be no mistake as to my stand on good music that was composed to be heard, listened to and enjoyed. The variety of music that is raucous, nasty, filled with foul language and abusive lyrics can find its way into any waste receptacle in America; I will not say a word, and for this I give you my golden word. *"Scouts Honor!" I Mean Really! I Will Not Say A Word!* But, I will celebrate with joy and thank The Creator that another person has raised from his or her sleep and embraced life and its value and purpose. When this happens, the world receives a gift that no one else could ever give. The gift is the gift of *your* true self and *you* expressing that to the world, free of façades and the mask of self-deception. I believe that, this section on *"Loud Music"* will be of great assistance to everyone, and younger people in general. I suggest that you read this chapter at least 3 times before moving on. The value of what has been said can easily be overlooked, but I guarantee that it will not be overlooked by life itself.

Chapter 20 How Are You Treating Life?

I often ask the question, *"How are you treating life?"* Instead of, "How is life treating you?" I have learned that life can only, and will only give you what you put into it. As has been stated throughout this book, *"You reap what you sow."* Life gives a fair reward; no one can escape the laws of nature that aid us in doing ourselves tremendous good or great harm. The choice is up to each and every one of us. We make these choices and when circumstances are not to our liking we often look outward. That is like going to the doctor for a stomach pain, and having the doctor look at other patients, and decides that their problems are your problems as well, even though he has not examined you! I do not think that such treatment would be satisfactory to you, but that is exactly what you do when you look outside for answers, while the cause is inside of you. Life is one big opportunity; your knowing and accepting this as fact will greatly increase and enhance your chances of attaining whatever your heart desires. How you treat life will determine what you get. By giving what you give, you open ways and means that have yet to be discovered by any human being before. It is my belief that the majority of people on earth do not fear death as much as they fear living! Most people believe that once the physical body dies that it is over. However, so many people die countless deaths by living in fear, doubt, suspicion and petty worry. Many people are fearful or dreadful of living, because they are afraid of what they might discover just in attempting something new and different for themselves.

Just like the story of the man on a ship who had been found guilty of a certain crime; the captain of the ship gave the convicted an alternative; "Either face the firing squad, or take what's behind that given door!" The captain gave the convicted twenty-four hours to think it over. After this time, the convicted chose the firing squad and was executed immediately. One of the officers asked the captain, "What was behind the door?" The captain answered, "Freedom." The man was afraid of what he did not know and chose death. Now, you may interpret this story any way you wish, however, I see it as one of the myriad examples of people who are afraid to live. Too many people would rather live with guilt, fear, doubt, negativity, crushing defeat and other things that are just as devastating, than to live, I mean really live and conquer fear; fear of Success is what it is called, and treating life as one big opportunity and living it that way, is a sure cure. Here is something that I recommend that everyone should do, "if you have not already done so, " Take your dictionary and cross out the following list of words. These words are what Napoleon Hill called enemies to success and Peace of Mind; *"Fear, Greed, Intolerance, Egotism, Lust, Anger, Hatred, Jealousy, Impatience, Deceit, Falsehood, Insincerity, Vanity, Cruelty, Mercilessness, Injustice, Slander, Gossip, Undependability, Dishonesty, Disloyalty, Revenge, Worry, Envy, Hypochondria, and Indecision."*

YOU MUST "HAVE" A DICTIONARY TO DO THIS! NOW IS THE PERFECT TIME TO INVEST A FEW DOLLARS IN ONE IF YOU DO NOT HAVE ONE!

Just by doing this little, "clearing exercise," your mind will start to operate from a different perspective. You have just instructed your subconscious mind which, *"is power without direction"* to discard and vanquish twenty-six major enemies to your life success and achievement of peace of mind and happiness. You must now follow the procedure with reading positive material, listening to uplifting motivational material, and keeping company with positive progressive minded people. Pray, Meditate, Think and establish a regular exercise routine. I here many people saying that they do not have time to read and listen to motivational and self-help material and that it does not work. I can say this with absolute certainty, "That type of negative thinking definitely works!" It works on the person that embraces that point of view. I find it interesting, and odd that people consider negative thinking more realistic and view positive thinking as daydreaming. That is called conditioning to the negative! For example; getting a job and living from pay check to pay check is realistic and being an entrepreneur is unrealistic. Why? I think that it is because of negative conditioning, and low self-esteem. Remember this, and you will be on firm ground, *"Any thing the mind can conceive and believe; the human mind can achieve."* People who tend to have negativity in their lives accept and breathe negativity. People who are successful tend to accept and breathe success and positive things. *How*

Are You Treating Life? Life is great and full of opportunities for each of us, but many are nasty and negative to it!

"However mean your life is, meet it and live it; do not shun it and call it hard names. It is not so bad as you are. It looks poorest when you are richest. The faultfinder will find faults even in paradise. Love your life, poor as it is. You may perhaps have some pleasant, thrilling, glorious hours, even in a poor-house." Thoreau

So you see, life is kind, gentle, firm, glorious and all the things that greatness, humility love and happiness are made of. It is never hard and mean! When we use our imaging powers of mind to create something different, and counter to peace, love, tranquility and true life success, we gather things that make us sad and unhappy and keep us from the eternal calm of the mind. When someone asks me, "How is life treating you?" I reply, "Super, great, fantastic and just wonderful!" Why? Life can only give me the best. I may have just lost my job or gotten into a car collision, but what does that have to do with, "how life is treating me?" Treat life with the respect that it deserves, and it will reward you with what you deserve and more than you can imagine. So, don't knock at the door and say, *"Let me in, let me in!"* Knock on the door and say, *"here is what I bring to life for the betterment of all life."* Life rewards the doers, those who use their gifts, time and talents along with their hearts to serve humanity. Life has nothing for selfish, egotistical individuals who only seek self-gratification and praise. Life praises and gratifies the unselfish, the giving and peace-loving individual all the days of their lives.

Things do not change, but we change! You can do what you desire, but keep your good thoughts, your wholesome, clean and successful thoughts and you will fare well in the great *"Game of Life."* The game of life is about one day at a time, one accomplishment at a time, and one project at a time. Success in the great game of life is measured in small achievements and big achievements. However, small or big, they are all the same. One achievement may take more time, money, and effort to finalize, but, all achievement signal success and triumph! Life is one big triumph after another, but each big triumph is usually a series of small victories over time. Life is fair, just, and balanced; therefore, the question remains, *"How Are You Treating Life?"* That question may lead you to a world beyond your most ardent desires if you ponder the question; really think and even write down things that come to mind. A good time to ask your self this question is early in the morning, before the birds get up, and before the sun begins to rise. You will discover the ease of thought flow when all is quiet and peaceful. You will discover that your thoughts dance with a sort of romantic delight with nature. Suddenly you will hear the chirp of birds and to your surprise; *(Hopefully to your delight)* they will be right outside your door or window. This happens to me every morning that I greet the day in anticipation of the miracle of the day. I have, on many occasions, greeted the day and creation with spoken words such as, *"Hello world, it's a great day and I am glad to be apart of it!"* This is not cheese time, or fill the pages of a book time; this is what I do, and have done for years. The effect that it has had on my life is immeasurable. My attitude is *strong, fair and just because* of it. Now, if I were to say to what extent that greeting the world has help me, "I would be guilty of filling the pages of a book," as I have no way of knowing except to say, *"Try it, and you might like it."*

What Is Your Life?

Have you ever thought about it! Have you ever stopped long enough to ask yourself, "What is my life?" There is no doubt in my mind that, few people will ever ask this question of themselves; a question that might be the most important question of anyone's lifetime. Your life is a wonder, a piece of art with a song that is written to harmonize with everything else created. Your life is more than just the seeing, breathing, smelling and the other senses; your life is a sum total of everything mental, physical, moral, and spiritual. Your life is the intangibles that are not necessarily seen by the average person. What do I mean by intangible? I am talking about your self-expression, which no one has or will ever have like you. If someone were to write a book or a song about you today, what would it say or how will it read? What is the legacy that you plan to leave for others to learn from? What legacy will you leave for your family to point to? What story does your life tell? I am not talking about material things, the ephemeral things; instead, I am talking again about the intangibles. The answer to these questions will answer the most important question which is, *"What Is Your Life?"*

Be bold by writing out the legacy that you desire to leave to your family, the world and to the universe! Take it to the next level by writing down what you want others to say of you, and what you want others to read about you. You do not need to have dreams of fame and fortune to do this. You can just do it to leave a message to those close to you, or your immediate family. It is a shame that the graveyard is filled with people that took brilliance to the grave, when life gave them so much more to offer. Write down your legacy, your eulogy, your epithet and your story! What if your story saved thousands of lives, help the many disadvantage children around the world, or by inspiration, brought the cure for some horrible disease? *"What Is Your Life?"* This is an all important question, because the essence of your life goes on long after you have left this life experience. The master lives on, and only the space in time changes; they recreate in another place. There is magic in your life.

Prayer and Meditation

(Do You Understand the Process?)

Prayer and meditation are means of communicating with Infinite Intelligence or The Creator of all things or your Higher self. Through these means, we are able to direct our thoughts and concentration for the sole purpose of aligning ourselves with that great energy or power source that is limitless and all wise. While it has been explained that the subconscious is power without direction; it takes any and all orders given it by the conscious mind. The *Super Conscious or Higher Power,* which we call *God, or The Creator, Infinite Intelligence* and so on, is the developer and the fashioner of what is received by our subconscious mind. We choose what goes into our powerful subconscious mind or others choose for us. Whatever goes in and is allowed to take root will manifest, be it foul or clean. We have the ability to fashion and image what we desire, and everything starts with our imagination and our courage to use our imagination.

This brings us to Prayer and Meditation and how they are effective. Millions of people pray daily and never seem to get a hold on their lives or accomplish their hearts desires. I, for instance, have never been short on performing the physical acts of prayer, several times daily; yet when it came to the results, my life was reflecting something different. The question then becomes, "why, and how come?" I will express my views on this and hopefully shed some insight into the subject so that your prayer and meditation will be more rewarding and less ritual with no meaning to you. Although many will not admit it, their prayers and meditations are merely rituals and are rarely understood; If, this is the case, how can *Prayer and Meditation* be fully appreciated and utilized? Let us first seek to understand what we are doing and not simply follow the crowd or what the theologians say. I am convinced that most people do not have an inkling of how, and/or why prayer and meditation is so powerful and intriguing.

Theory of Prayer and Meditation

The belief is generally that if we pray and meditate, our prayer and meditations will soon bring about or manifest what we desire. More often than not, people fail to attain their heart's desire through these media. I believe that it not only boils down to belief and faith, but more importantly, knowingness, which are all important in the attainment of your desires. But, *understanding, over standing,* and *deep insight* into what is actually going on during the prayer or meditation period, is of paramount importance. The words uttered during the ritual and the focus of the prayer is key when backed by faith and a true desire. The words you say and the thoughts you think are being impressed upon your *subconscious mind* just as you would aim the lens of a camera in a certain direction and click! The picture is then taken and developed and given back to you just as *"you"* imagined it to be! *Read that last sentence again, because it may be the most important sentence, that many of you have read your entire life!* Let's put it this way, "Until you understand the process of prayer and meditation, in that you are saying words to impress them upon your subconscious mind, so that the *superconscious* or *The Creator* in you will receive it, and give it back to you with the perfect plan, you are merely uttering words!" Realization is manifestation! The words you speak are visualized or become mental images, and those imagined images, if kept in focus in your thoughts, will *"become"* that which you say! Once you have the deep faith, unwavering belief and knowingness in what you ask, seek and knock for; then you open the way for like minds and unseen forces to come to your aid. If you pray for perseverance and patience along with drive, and the will to keep seeking and taking action with this idea of prayer and meditation, you will without doubt, obtain the qualities you seek. You now know, that you have the power to be, do and have what you like to be, do and have. Knowing what you do not know is important and, knowing that you know, that you don't know, is the beginning of wisdom and enlightenment. That may sound a bit confusing to you, but, if you read it carefully, I have no doubt that it will turn on the lights in your mind. It is this, *"not knowing that you don't know,"* that keeps so many people living lives unfulfilled and full of idle wishes. I am convinced that if you knew, prior to reading this, that when you pray and meditate; the things you say, are said to instill in you, the *"qualities"* necessary to attract to your reality that which you seek, whether spiritual, mental, moral or otherwise. Further, you would not only have stronger faith, you would definitely have answered prayers and meditation periods. This is the gift of imaging and the love shown to us by whom I call God. Don't you feel better, knowing that when you pray you can get up knowing that you are like a photographer, taking the pictures that you desire to manifest in your life? You must *know* this for it to manifest; if you do not *know* this, you cannot have sufficient faith in the process, and therefore you become a merely ritual person. *Prayer and Meditation works!* You have to know that it works and why! I am not saying that you must adopt my thoughts on the subject to succeed; I am saying that you will definitely gain an increase in what you desire. Prayer and meditation only works because YOU DO!

Man means *mind,* and you have complete control over your mind, your thoughts and your speech! You are not your mind! You are much more than the flesh and bones that you may think that you are. You may *fashion, design and/or structure* your life the way you desire, but only if you understand that what you ask for from the *Creator, God (or by whatever excellent name you call him,)* is in your hands to imagine and shape. All things are answered immediately. The unseen things which you have no control of, is not your department; that is the department of *God, or the Higher power,* and he will take care and make things happen. Some of these happenings may appear to be mere coincidences, but they will aid you and bring you into contact with just what you needed. Those so called coincidences are God's way of staying announced in your mind! Now when you pray or meditate, think of it in this way, and watch how confident and peaceful you will feel. *Knowing* that the words you say are actually instructions to your subconscious mind or soul, giving you strength and a whole new insight into yourself and your God given ability. I am not talking about religion, (That is not what I do!) I am speaking of the power of the *words* you speak and the *thoughts* that you think! Here is the key, *"In the beginning was the word, and the word was God, and the word became manifested in the flesh."* Taken from, the *Holy Bible*. How about this one, "*God taught man utterance (words) and speech."* Taken from the *Holy Qur'an.* There are many plain and clear passages in many scriptures in all ages and countries, which say essentially the same thing. The rules do not change because of *race, creed, skin color, religion, geographical location, education, height, weight, or for the richest or the poorest people on earth!* The rules are the same no matter what you profess or do not profess. Therefore, there are no advantages, except for the one who utilizes this powerful resource even if his understanding of this concept is most basic. This is what makes prayer and meditation so powerful; this is also why so many people pray, and attend services around the world; yet seem to come up empty handed, while looking for some miraculous happening outside. Miracles are real; they come from the *inside* of you! Your words, and thoughts, spoken and unspoken along with assistance from the Creator, Infinite Intelligence or God, is what makes it all work. Let the light of understanding shine in your heart today and you will make a better way. As for belief in God; I am well aware of the fact that some people do not believe in a God or what have you, that are perfectly fine with me, but in spite of this, *"the rules of the mind, words and thoughts, don't change!"*

Imagination and Ideas

What is imagination? My good friend Langston Hughes asked me, "*What happens to a dream deferred? Does it dry up like a raisin in the sun?"* What about ideas? Do they come when we need them or do they just come and go without rhyme or reason? What about imagination? Are our images merely an inner television without purpose? Imagination is the minds oil and lubricant, and in it are molded all agenda for accomplishment. Ideas are the genius in all of us, and it is waiting for expression and release into the greater universe. Do you not know that the beginning of winning, and of achievement, is bound by what you imagine and what ideas you allow to prosper and develop in your mind? Ideas do not come to you for any reason. They come for food, shelter, comfort and acknowledgment. How do you feed, shelter and acknowledge an idea? You use it, act on it, bring it to reality and make it service others. You image what you desire, you get ideas which harmonize with your desire, and your imagination goes to work on that idea. If you act on what you imagine, you will have found that winning is not for the few fortunate individuals, but winning, achieving, or advancing is also for you.

A great and well-respected man of history once said, *"I have learned that success is to be measured not so much by the position that one has reached in life as by obstacles which he has overcome trying to succeed."* That man was born a slave, but died as one of the greatest minds the world has, and will possibly ever know! That man was, **Booker Taliaferro Washington,** who established the Tuskegee Institute, one of the finest schools in the history of the United States of America. His accomplishments are truly a marvel of time, if you consider that blacks were not allowed to read for over 300 years, when, suddenly came freedom for a little boy who lived outside the box; out of his imagination, and did not listen to those who said he couldn't. As a little boy, Booker T, Washington worked in a dark coal mine. He imagined learning to read and became educated. He used the power of his imagination, which in turn attracted the ideas needed to develop what he imaged, and greatness was the result!

We are here to achieve, and we are here to achieve repeatedly. Ideas are fuel for our imagination, and imagination with effort gives birth to achievement. Ideas are the diamonds and gold, rubies and pearls we have been looking for. Ideas and the imagination are the sparks are the fortune we so often look outside of ourselves for. We do not need some quick fix scheme or some Hollywood discovery to make our lives different. All we need to know is how to exercise our ideas, and our imagination, to achieve. If you wish to make yourself a more attractive package, a more disciplined or enthusiastic person, then, *"stand inside yourself!"* As Dr. Norman Vincent Peale once said, *"See the Possibilities!"* The greatest possibilities for you are right there, where you stand, sleep and eat. Now, do the groundwork; the foundation must be poured; build the structure of your life! No one will ever blame you for trying, but, you will blame yourself one thousand times, for not going *inside yourself,* and working with your ideas and imagination to achieve. Helen Keller was blind and deaf before she reached the tender young age of 2 years old, and yet she went on to be an inspiration to blind and deaf people all over the world. She had an imagination, and that is where she lived, because that is all that she had. She could have given up and no one would have blamed her, but she went on and became one of the greatest pioneers this country has ever seen. She was admired by great contemporaries like, Alexander Bell, Samuel Clemens, world leaders, and the great industrialist, Andrew Carnegie, just to name a few. A deaf, blind young lady became a giant among giants. Why? Because she had courage! She utilized the gift of imagination, which attracted to her reality the ideas necessary for her accomplishments in life. Helen Keller's life is the story of your life; *"Can you see the endless possibilities?"*

Chapter 21 I Am
(The State Of Being)

The boomerang effect: Sooner or later, what we speak and think comes back to us. What we become is what we think about with a burning desire or persistence in our minds and hearts. Karma, which is Sanskrit for "comeback," says, "What you sow, you will reap." Now this has been said many ways throughout the ages and it is true! It is also known as, "*The Law of Cause and Effect.*"

"*I Am*" is that great being, fashioned by the mighty hand of God, who governs all things and needs nothing. "*I Am*" is that brilliant conqueror of fear, doubt, lack and scarcity created by our own minds. *I Am* is that man of dynamic and spectacular wealth that is my / our divine right and inheritance. *I Am* is that giver of goods and services for the betterment of society. *I am what I am,* because, "I say so, do so; therefore I am so." *I Am What I Am. I Am* self-improved. Self-improvement is the key; it unlocks the door. Self-improvement is the gate keeper, the palace guard, the magic elixir of life. Things material, are testimony to *"what we are, and what we have become."*

Our goals and their attainment are the measure of our self-improvement. As we liberate ourselves, from lack, loss and limitation, and become that which we desire; those things that we desire come to us with blinding speed and accuracy. It is this state of *"I Am Ness,"* that is important and, not the things that we desire to create, be they physical or mental. Whether in business, or any part of life; *Being-ness*, is the state that says, *"I Am." I Am* all that I desire to be and do all I desire to do, now! Not tomorrow, but now, in the midst of myself. *I Am,* is the place where greatness resides, where the artist paints and the song writer writes. *I Am* is the place that communicates to others, *"I Am comfortable with who and what I have become." "I Am What I Am."* I Am a product of my own imagination, out of that grand image created in the likeness of *"The Creator,"* Therefore, *"I Am!"* The image and imagination are correlated. Out of the Imagination, or image that "*The Creator"* has put in us, we have the power to become, therefore, *"to Be."* Once we can *be or become*, then we can declare , "*I Am, What I Am,"* with alacrity and assurance. This is powerful and dynamic, real and awesome. Many people search for life's jewels *without*, while neglecting what is *within.* You cannot grow within and stand still without. I am, you are, centuries and millenniums of thoughts, things and ideas. Once you "*BE or Become,*" you are, *"I AM."* You become *"One"* with that supply of all power, of all things imaginable to man. You tap into that river that flows at the gate of paradise. "*I Am What I Am."* You need no approval nor hearty praise nor uplifting from outside, all you need is to decide that *you are,* then declare, *"I Am What I Am."* That is the most profound position from which a human being can operate. It is the only position that can give you that fruitful moment in time. All we have is one moment in time. The next moment is the only moment and so on.

Because I have decided to be, at this moment, right now, *I am what I Am*. We can remain the same or change what we are by what we think about in our minds and hearts. There is no other course; there is only power in the *"I AM."* And what about that deviant called *"opinions of others?"* The opinion on the inside is far more important, and, it is that one, that determines the quality of life.

"I Am", is a place where you exude class and charisma; you radiate confidence, poise and calmness of character. *I Am* is a state of arrival and assurance in yourself and life's deposits back to you. When you are in this state, you walk with a gait that says, *I Am* more than somebody, I help mold, and develop other bodies. *I Am,* is a place where you feel totally unselfish in your giving of your time, energy, money and love. You are the leader that others see, hear, feel, taste and smell, because you are at one with yourself. You are the man or the woman, this is your hour, and you are the marquis! You are not the marquis because you are an egotistical, self-serving (at others demise) creature. You are the marquis because of your genuine *"I Am ness;"* your willingness to share and maintain that position of *"positive power."* You are willing to share with others to become like God; You are a being of transformational sharing. *I Am What I Am.*

So many people spend their entire lives never realizing that special place, where the "*Isles Of Blessedness*" awaits your coming. Finally, but not final, *"I Am,"* is an attitude of gratitude to the Creator of all things, for all things and a life of service to others, to show our appreciation for having been given the privilege to walk this great planet. *"I Am ness,"* communicates to others that we understand what it means to *"be in the will of The Creator."* To serve mankind, is to be in the *will o*f the Great God, *"The Creator of All Things." Be calm and poised, stay humble.* Henry David Thoreau wrote; *"Humility like darkness reveals the heavenly lights." He also wrote, "Things do not change, we change." I AM NESS*, changes people, places and things; "*I AM*" says, "Come and I will make you believers in *"self,"* therefore in a higher power." *I AM* says, "You are more than what you have become; I can assist you in getting to where you desire to go in your heart and soul." *I AM* is a state of love and certainty of your special place in life and its perfect expression. *I AM is directly connected with "Universal Power and Peace!"*

Daring To Be

A young 12 year old telephoned Bill Hewlett, the founder of Hewlett Packard, and asked for the spare parts for computers. He had a vision and a dream and boldness to go with it. How many older people, would think of approaching a successful business man and founder of the Hewlett Packard Corporation, and asking for help. Yet, at the age of 12, Steve Jobs did so. Later he met Steve Wozniak and together they designed and built a computer, the *Personal Computer.* Steve Jobs founded Apple Computer, which became a great success. At the moment Steve

Jobs had phoned Bill Hewlett with his request, his soul was saying, *"I Am!"* Steve Jobs operated from *"I Am Ness."* By the time he was 25 years old or so, he was a multi-millionaire. Make no mistake about it, *"He became,"* therefore *"He received."* In the first person, Steve Jobs would say, *"I Am."* The journey was exciting and thrilling because he experienced the process of *Being Ness*, and *I Am Ness.*

The Tree is a tree, The Bird is a bird, The Whale is a whale, but the human *"Being,"* can choose *to be* whatever! *What we think about, that we are.* We can fly like a bird and even higher and faster, we can swim the ocean like a Whale, (in a ship) but faster and more efficiently. We can spread our branches like a tree, but farther and higher and stronger than any tree. We can and we must continue to be and declare, *"I AM!"* Declare it with humility, not for show or for someone else, but for the fact that we are. Others will see it without us ever speaking a word of it. *I AM Ness* dominates your mind body and soul. If you hid its light under a bush, it would burn the entire planet up. That is one of the secrets or mysteries of the *"Burning Bush"* that Moses saw and heard; *"I Am."* As in the case of Moses, if you have been sent by *"I Am,"* who can stop you? Moses *became,* therefore he conquered and lead his people to freedom. "Tell them, *I Am* sent you." God was going to deliver the people, but they needed to take action. He, through Moses, told them what they must do. God was not humiliated, beaten, and enslaved, "the people were," and they had to become one with *"I Am Ness,"* to alleviate that situation.

The reason that I am saying this is, "People wait for it to be done for them through prayer or meditation and affirmation. While there is great power in these, and I certainly love all three, prayer mediation and affirmations, "I understand that the action that must precede them is the planting in the soil." Whatever you ask of life, it will give you, but you must make your actions in accord with what you desire and walk upright from then to your desired goal.

A great poet stated, *"I bargained with life for a penny, and life would pay no more, however I begged at evening when I counted my scanty store. For life is a just employer, he gives you what you ask, but once you have set the wages, why, you must bear the task. I worked for a menial's hire, only to learn, dismayed, that any wage I had asked of life, life would have willingly paid."*

"I Am, and Being Ness," is true freedom. Thoreau wrote; *"If one advances confidently in the direction of his dreams, and endeavors to live the life which he has imagined, he will meet with a success unexpected in common hours. He will put some things behind, will pass an invisible boundary; new, universal and more liberal laws will begin to establish themselves around and within him; or the old laws be expanded, and interpreted in his favor in a more liberal sense, and he will live with the license of a higher order of beings. In proportion as he simplifies his life, the laws of the universe will appear less complex, and solitude will not be solitude, nor poverty,*

poverty, nor weakness, weakness. If you have built castles in the air, your work need not be lost; that is where they should be. Now put the foundation under them."

"I Am and Being Ness," says that you are lined up with the universe and the vast resources available. No man can exhaust those resources no matter how intelligent, smart and wise we become. *"New Laws,"* will be interpreted in your favor and you will live with the license of a higher order of Beings. This is one of the most profound statements that I have ever heard. When you go for your goals, dreams and desires and you go forth with alacrity, drive and determination, boundaries expand, things happen that you do not expect; people cross your path that would have never found you, and the universe will create something new, just for you and no one can adequately explain it. That is why we read stories and hear about famous people who faced all kinds of odds and even though things were against them, they went on to become some of the greatest people in our history. There is something beyond what "we know;" there are greater powers at work for every one of us. There are laws, universal laws that will be created just to fit your circumstance, your time, and your specific calling, which no one else can call on but you.

A Plan "Be"

Someone said, "People don't plan to fail, they fail to plan." The greatest plan that you can have is to *"Be."* What is everything else but a result, or an effect without, from what flows from within? It is imperative for you to *"Plan to Be."* Your knowledge got you where you are today, so what makes you think that your knowledge, without a *Plan to Be*, can take you further on the road "*To Become?"* To *"Be"* requires that you study, seek, ask questions, look for mentors and role models to learn from, and follow their good, and sound examples. To "Be" requires that you dig deep within and be introduced to your *other self.* Without this digging and mining for the gold that is within you, a state of "*Being Ness"* is merely a wish and will never materialize in your life.

There is life beyond having little material possessions. You can lose your car, home, job, and even your family and still operate to get to where you desire to go. Those material things are great, but you have to *"Become"* to have. Not *"Becoming,"* before you can *have* is like asking the ground for the harvest and then promising to plant the seed later. Having and a "*Plan Be,"* is much like farming; you decide what crop you desire and then you make the necessary preparations to the ground and plant the seeds of your ardent desire. The farmer knows the approximate time of harvest, which is usually *not in the same season as the planting.* The farmer understands the seasons, the animals and insects that threaten the harvest, and the market for his products. The vegetables and fruits that you enjoy are the direct result of the farmer having a plan. The proof is in your stomach! The proof of your personal, "*Plan to Be,*" is in your life and in every aspect of it. You can not hide it or conceal it in any manner as there will always be those who understand this, *"We Become What We Think About."* This is ageless wisdom and many wise people know this to be a fact.

You do not have to plan failure or mediocrity. Mediocre is always ready and willing to serve you and so is failure. You need no books tapes or seminars on how to fail. You need no knowledge of the workings of the human mind or mentors or role models. You need not put forth any effort in becoming mediocre or a failure. In fact, others will bring the thing to you and most people readily accept it. There are neither applications nor resumes, no proof of being a failure is required and no references ever needed. Anyone can be a failure or be mediocre and never have to show proof of their *failure or mediocre experience.* But, *"To Be,"* that is the question! To be more, stronger, better, marvelous, great, grand and soaring like an Eagle, you must "*Become*" all that you can become. Who do you study? What role models in your field do you listen to, study and learn from? What books do you read, and how much time do you spend listening to tapes and reading biographies of others. How many people can you name in your field of interest who are successful and have the level of success that you desire to acquire? What actions are you taking daily to achieve your goals? How many times a day do you read, think about and ponder your affirmations. How many hours per week do you sit in a quiet place and think and write down the ideas that come to you? How often do you enjoy the peace and calmness of your own being, in your soul, all by yourself? What is your definite purpose, your *Clear Vision* of where you are going and what you are becoming? What are your immediate goals? What goals have you set to accomplish daily, weekly, monthly, quarterly, yearly, or 5 and 10 year from now? What are your 15 and 20 year goals? Most of you have not thought about it and many of you that have, have never taken the time to write them out and get them out of your imagination and into action. Remember this, "*The use of the pen is clocked into your genes, or our being. The pen is mightier than the sword and the ink of a scholar is holier than the blood of a martyr.* Every thing that we produce, as human beings, emanate from our minds and the minds of others. When we use the pen and put it to paper, we not only see it to remind us, but we also give it life and vitality, by reading the plans and ideas everyday. It is easier to give birth than to raise the dead. Once we create our desire, we put them to paper to give them life; our application, practice and constant action nourishes them, make them stronger until they have their own legs, and are sufficient to provide a service for the world. *Someone said, "you cannot travel within and stand still without."* A strong enough desire, will lead you to write them down, then you will have reinforcement on the outside to achieve your desire.

"Let the Master within you roam freely, and the world will reward you for even the simplest intelligence."

Conclusion

Some Final Words

It has been a ride, a joy and a privilege writing this material. I sure loved expressing my thoughts and words, and sharing some of my personal experiences with you. I have been with you for a little over 90 days, writing, thinking, receiving inspiration to write, and just smiling because of the beauty that I feel in my heart. You may not know me personally, yet with every stroke of my keyboard, "you were in my mind." It has been like a little child playing at the park or blowing out birthday candles. I am that happy with my life and myself. Recently I was at the park with my children and my son wanted an ice cream, when the thought came to me, *"This is what it is all about."* I was buying ice cream for my children, on a sunny day, at the park. That thought, just lights up my soul, and causes it to dance the day and night away. I have never felt this way before. Big accomplishments in life are all great and well worth going for, but, I pray to God that I never loose the joy and happiness of the little things. What can be more joyous than buying children ice cream on a sunny day in the park, and having one for your self too? What can be more intriguing than wondering what rainbows taste like, or if the sun tastes like orange juice? Do the clouds taste like milk and honey? Is the moon one big lump of cheese? My imagination is working just fine and I love every bit of it. Money does not burn a hole in my pocket as it used to. I am comfortable with money; it does not define me and it does not enslave me. I can have any amount of money that one can have, and still feel like a little child at heart. The greatest value in you is that little child in you which is full of love, peace, light and happiness. Please do not be ashamed to love like a child; you might seriously want to consider visiting your past and freeing the child in you, *if you have not already done so."* I wish I could give you the feeling and the bliss, but you know that I cannot do that. Besides, that would be "cheating you" out of the experiences and the stories that you have to share with others and me. I assure you that there is no story that is more rewarding than *your* own personal story. Release it and let the world feel the beauty in you. The Master is knocking at your door, "the door inside your heart." While reading this book, and even at this very moment, you are literally, "ONE MINUTE TO HEALTHY ESTEEM."

Tamir Qadree
(With Gary)
www.esteemnow.com

Wonderful

*Wonderful thoughts, dreams and all;
They are what they seem, they are that
gleam in your eye.*

*Wonderful character, announces its aim,
its purpose and flame. Wonderful you are;
The sun shines in you, to yourself be true!*

*Wonderful, how your personality embraces
Reality, and brings charm, charisma and class
to all in mass.*

*Stay Wonderful as you naturally are!
And the beauty that only you can
Inspire, will take you higher.*

*Wonderful; you are wonderful, you are that
Jewel. You are the laughter,
You are the love of the world.
You are forever wonderful*

About The Author

Your grandparents and parents heard the works of the great *Dr. Norman Vincent Peale, Earl Nightingale, Jim Rohn, Zig Ziglar* and the likes. Your Parents have listened to the motivational, superbly delivered style of *Les Brown*, the marketing genius that embodies *Anthony Robbins*; the powerful simplicity of *Robert Kiyosaki* and his Rich Dad, Poor Dad diamonds. Now, it's your time to feel, see, hear and experience the new, exciting and wondrous world of Tamir Qadree! With Tamir Qadree, there is only one question to ask your self, and only one! The question is, *"Are You An Observer?"* Tamir Qadree is an Author, Speaker and Dynamic Success / Life Coach. He currently resides in the beautiful state of California. The love, peace, hopes, and passion that he inspires is not only contagious, but his style is *inimitable and new!* He will energize you and enlighten you all in the same breath. Tamir Qadree has a passion for assisting and developing others, through his books, live engagements, and audio products. Tamir Qadree has known his life's "calling or perfect self-expression," since he was thirteen years old, and probably much younger. When it comes to the art of speaking, assisting others and writing, he is simply *"In his element, because, he is the element as you are your element."* Tamir Qadree is an outrageous; go out on the limb, out of the box thinker! Tamir Qadree will often observe old sayings, quotes and deep beliefs, that he believes hinders many from their *God* given rights, which are, *"Good health, abundant wealth, true love and true life calling."*

To learn more about products and services offered by Tamir Qadree, visit www.esteemnow.com,
Or email: tamir@esteemnow.com

Please Mail All inquires and product orders to;

Esteem Now, Inc.
6333 Pacific Ave Suite 525
Stockton CA. 95207.

Jeffery Combs

Jeffery Combs, president of Golden mastermind Seminars, Inc. is an internationally recognized speaker, trainer and author. He specializes in prospecting, leadership, personal breakthroughs, prosperity consciousness, spiritual enlightenmnet, mindset training and effective marketing. His training revolves around personal growth and development, cuts to the chase, and delivers information that immediately impacts your success!

Jeff is the author of the highly inspiring book and audio series, "More Heart Than Talent," along with numerous other motivational and personal develoment products. He has personally consulted with thousands of clients in his coaching career, and is committed to assisting people change the way they feel in order to achieve their goals and dreams.

Jeff is available for consulting, mentoring, and personal one on one coaching. his professional guidance will assist you to create maximum results now!

For further information, Please call 800-595-6632 or visit his website at www.GoldenMastermind.com.

Erica Combs

Erica Combs is the Vice President of Golden Mastermind Seminars, Inc. and an internationally recognized speaker, author and trainer. Her experience in free enterprise combined with her personal growth has allowed her to step into her power and assist her clients to reconnect with their power & brilliance to create quantum changes in their enterprises and in their lives!

Based upon her personal experience, Erica can assure you first-hand that success as an entrepreneur requires an entirely different level of self-esteem, communication, focus and permission than most people are taught is acceptable by their families, co-workers and peers. Success will require that you begin to examine your current beliefs and give yourself permission to release those which no longer serve you so that you may adopt new and empowering beliefs to lead you to manifesting your dreams.

Erica's coaching and training focuses on creating a foundation for you to begin your journey to personal power, and to create an anchor you can use to reconnect with your internal peace as you continue your journey of personal development in the land of free enterprise.

Erica is available for consulting, mentoring, and personal one on one coaching. Her professional guidance will assist you to create maximum results now! Erica doesn't teach theory - she teaches the same skills she uses in business so you can begin creating the results you desire in free enterprise today!

For further information, please call 800-595-6632 or visit her website at www.goldenmastermind.com.